all color book of *Butterflies*

Robert Goodden

Octopus
Octopus Books

Contents

Introduction 5
The Fascination of Butterflies 6
European Butterflies 10
African Butterflies 22
North American Butterflies 32
South American Butterflies 40
Asian Butterflies 52
Butterflies of the Australian Region 64
Acknowledgments 72

First published in 1973 by
Octopus Books Limited,
59 Grosvenor Street, London W 1

© Octopus Books Limited

ISBN 0 7064 0231 6

Distributed in the U.S.A. by Crescent Books,
a division of Crown Publishers, Inc.

Produced by Mandarin Publishers Limited,
77a Marble Road, North Point, Hong Kong
Printed in Hong Kong

Introduction

People planning a trip to a distant country often like to know what sorts of butterflies they may see while there, and in this book I have tried to give a glimpse of the butterflies that are to be found all over the world, selecting them from a cross section of the major families on each continent. In each case I have given at least a mention, and in many cases, quite a good idea of the range that can be expected, although the range will vary with the season, of course.

Butterflies should be thought of as living things, not as specimens, nor objects for a collection to be accumulated in sets. This approach may be difficult for a European collector who is likely never to be able to travel to the tropics and remote islands and who is not really interested in breeding butterflies, especially when he can see the gorgeous specimens in reference works. There is not a great deal of information about most tropical butterflies and the collector may be forgiven for not always realizing to what extent butterflies' life histories, and their colours and shapes, are affected by the local terrain and ecology and the interrelationships of the species that fly with them. It is essential to consider how butterflies live, what they feed on and how they come to exist in one particular place rather than another, in order to appreciate them fully.

Because of this, as many butterflies as possible are shown living in their natural surroundings, with texts that briefly explain their relationships and individual characteristics. Plates of set specimens have been included to show a wider cross section from each continent, but there are still many fine species for which no room could be found. This book is intended to serve as a brief guide to anyone beginning to study or collect butterflies; but above all, my aim has been to show how wonderful the world of butterflies is, not just for the entomologist, but for everyone.

Over Compton, Sherborne, Dorset.   R G

The Fascination of Butterflies

I find it rather hard to define exactly what it is about butterfl
that makes them such an absorbing interest, not only for you
people but indeed for adults as well throughout a lifetime. Th
initial attraction, there can be no doubt, lies in their glowi
brilliant colours and patterns. Few creatures in the anim
kingdom can match the brilliant colouring and perfect shape
the incredible Birdwings from New Guinea, the depth
iridescent blue of the South American Morpho butterflies or
beauty of the silver spangles and jewel-like markings on
Lycaenidae from all parts of the world.

As a child of four I can remember watching Tortoiseshe
and Cabbage Whites in our garden. Their fascination for
must have arisen chiefly from curiosity, mixed with the attra
tion of their beautiful patterning and also the way they dart
about from flower to flower, defying all my attempts to cat
them in my cupped hands. This feeling of excitement at watc
ing butterflies never left me and I soon started to bu
up an interesting collection.

This is the way most children start their interest in butterfli

with a net. And I don't think this should be condemned because it is the one way a child can understand how to go out watching and finding butterflies, and he will quickly learn how fragile they are. The fun and excitement of chasing them appeals to children and leads them on to an interest in the butterfly families. I well remember going out, at the age of eight, on caterpillar collecting expeditions. I would knock on the doors of nearly all the houses with large gardens in my home villages of Over and Nether Compton in Dorset, and ask their owners whether I might look for caterpillars. Later, imagining their enthusiasm matched my own, I would invite these kind people round to see my caterpillar collection, all in labelled jam jars. Little did I think that one day I would have my own butterfly farm nearby and live in one of those houses with a lovely garden where I would be breeding thousands of butterflies every year.

However, one doesn't have to be all serious about it. There is no harm in appreciating butterflies for their beauty without feeling it necessary to study them in scientific depth. It is not a sin to collect butterflies just because they are beautiful and interesting and have fascinating stories attached to them. There are some people who would not admit to this strong aesthetic attraction and claim that their interest is wholly scientific. Have a look at their collection, though, and see whether it does not have a strong bias towards the brighter-coloured families.

Collections help us to study butterflies and work out their correct identifications and relationships. They are necessary, and there is also a great deal to be learnt from making expeditions to all kinds of habitats and countryside to watch and collect butterflies. It is great fun, too, as well as being good for the health. But there are great pressures on butterflies from man these days, pressures that are not coped with by the normal, existing forms of protection, such as mimicry. Butterflies are used to putting up with eternal danger and predation but they cannot survive the destruction of their habitats by the cutting down of their food plants, the planting of coniferous forest in place of deciduous woodland, the ploughing over of wasteland and the extension of building and agriculture, not just in Europe

but on every other continent as well. This destruction of habitats is more than a threat; it has already caused serious declines in numbers and species. British butterflies are becoming quite scarce by old standards: gone are the days of huge colonies of Chalkhill and Adonis Blues at Royston and Folkestone, and all over the country other downland butterflies are disappearing.

Collecting therefore must be kept within very well-considered limits and the old practice of having hundreds of specimens of a single species (several drawers full) in a collection must not continue. Species which have been reduced to such small colonies that they can hardly survive must not be collected at all. On the contrary, in fact, we should look at a species in such circumstances, study it closely and see whether there is anything we can do to help it to survive and maybe even increase itself again. The Large Blue butterfly in Britain is in just such a predicament; its numbers have dwindled terrifyingly, yet collectors are still trying to take specimens. The few remaining, very localized areas where colonies can be found have to be kept secret. Because of the Large Blue's curious life cycle, which requires its larvae to live in ants' nests, it is very difficult to raise in captivity. But we believe that if this were possible we could release quantities of butterflies in the flight season and build up the colonies once again. Experimental work on this is being undertaken by myself and my wife Rosemary at Over Compton, in conjunction with the British Butterfly Conservation Society. Some progress has been made and a method developed for keeping the larvae in ants' nests indoors. By watching the species and studying its localities in England and abroad very closely we have learnt a great deal about the Large Blue, including its use of an entirely new food plant (Marjoram) not previously recorded. Such close studies of similar endangered species cou greatly help them and prevent their decline or even extinctio

Everyone concerned about the conservation of butterfli can do a lot to help by joining their local county naturalis trust or conservation society, and taking an active part in i work. Those with gardens and farms can restrict and control th use of chemicals on their land, deliberately allowing some wi patches and hedges to remain there; city dwellers can help b encouraging others to be interested in conserving our butterfli

Many entomologists, of course, do not have collections at a Much of their interest lies in butterfly watching, in the insec natural haunts. Photographs enable us to share the exciteme of seeing a butterfly in its natural surroundings. Good pictur demand a reasonably good camera but a lot can be done wi any single-lens reflex 35 mm camera, using extension tub rather than expensive special lenses. Seeing butterflies at su close quarters gives us vital information about their habits a ecology, which we must have in order to help conserve the Strange as it may seem, we are still ignorant of a mass of small facts about even the commonest species.

Many species can be bred in captivity and I think this is o of the most exciting ways of enjoying butterflies. There a several books which outline methods of rearing butterflies a moths and it is surprising how many can be kept quite happi in environments and on food plants that they are not accu tomed to. You can go out and find your own caterpillars, eg and chrysalides, or buy native and foreign species too fro butterfly breeders. The thrill of watching the emergence of perfect butterfly that you have reared yourself, right throu from the egg, is really something to be experienced.

evious pages, left: A Peacock
nbathing on autumn flowers in
eparation for hibernation. This is one
 Europe's prettiest butterflies and they
e especially noticeable late in the year
hen they flock to the last garden
owers to store up energy for the winter.
 the late summer and autumn, you can
tract Peacocks by the dozen, together
ith Tortoiseshells, Painted Ladies and
ed Admirals, by planting your garden
ith plenty of the right flowers. The
e plant, *Sedum spectabile*, is especially
od. In September one plant can attract
 many as 40 or 50 butterflies at a time.
ichaelmas daisy, valerian, African
arigold, buddleia and catmint are all
ry attractive to these butterflies.
ne caterpillars of the Peacock butterfly
ed on stinging nettle, so be sure to
ave some wild patches and encourage
ndowners to do the same so that these
tterflies will continue to visit.

evious pages, right: There is much fun
 be had and much information to be
learnt from making expeditions to
different types of habitats and
countryside to watch or bring back
butterflies for a collection. But remember
that butterflies are under great pressure
from destruction of their habitats by
man. This beautiful Alpine scene in
Austria shows the sort of flowery
meadowland, high in the mountains,
which butterflies like. The slope has
been cut for hay but many parts are left
and almost no crop spraying is done here.
Butterflies abound and are in no danger
as long as the countryside remains
unspoilt and undeveloped.

Left: This photograph, the first colour
picture of a Large Blue caterpillar
published to date, shows the inside of an
ant colony that is living inside a walnut
shell. Queen, workers and brood are
occupying the crevices along with the
Large Blue caterpillar in its own chamber
which it has lined with a thin layer of
its own spun silk. This is where it rests
for the winter. This nest is part of a
project to rear the Large Blue in captivity
and to learn more about its habits. This
species has seldom been successfully
raised because of its complicated
relationship with ants. But the Large Blue
is now in danger of extinction and we
hope that these close studies may enable
us to save this remarkable butterfly
whose life cycle is unique in Britain.

Above: Perhaps one of the most exciting
ways of enjoying butterflies is to breed
them at home where you can watch them
as they progress through all their
remarkable stages. These soft, velvety
green caterpillars are African Citrus
Swallowtails, *Papilio demodocus*. They
don't have to have their native food
plant, orange, but are feeding here on a
bush of mock orange, *Choisya ternata*,
in a greenhouse. This plant is a hardy
evergreen that is easy to grow, and the
larvae can be kept anywhere indoors.
Many exciting butterflies and moths
from all over the world can be raised at
home, often on common wild plants.

European Butterflies

Don't be misled into thinking that European butterflies are d
and uninteresting in comparison with tropical species. A coll
tion of European species has a charm and delicacy that ma
any outside the Palearctic region (this region extends across
northern hemisphere and includes part of China and all
Japan, where the species are closely allied to those found
Europe: many, in fact, are the same). Consider for interest,
climatic effects of latitudes which range from true Arctic c
down to the desert heat of northern Africa, the contr
between the snowy altitudes of the Alps, and the marshy pla
of central Europe and the variation both in climate and terr
between the seaswept Atlantic coasts to the west and the a
mountainous areas bordering Asia Minor in Turkey and Gree
Obviously, Europe must have, and indeed does have, an
tremely varied and scientifically important butterfly fauna.

Iceland has no indigenous butterflies at all. This might at fi
seem reasonable because of the scarcity of trees and bushes, b
it is less so when one reads the impressive list of butterflies to
found right inside the Arctic Circle at latitudes even furth

orth, both in Europe and in America. There is a fascination out the Arctic species, probably because one cannot quite lieve that any butterflies, let alone so many, could withstand e harsh climate, with temperatures 10° below zero Centigrade, d snow for the greater part of the year. There is a curious, definable character about many of the species which are und only or mainly in the Arctic. Somehow they *look* Arctic: is may possibly have something to do with the overall pale or ghtly transparent effect of their colour. Who would think that e almost exotic Swallowtail *Papilio machaon*, has a stronghold at stretches to the northernmost limits of Norway and nland where it can exist in an adapted form *P.m. laponnicus.* e Painted Lady which is hatched in Africa, migrates right up these parts, and so do Tortoiseshells, Camberwell Beauties, mmon Blues, Green Hairstreaks and others. Only a little rther south the Brimstone, Orange Tip and the Fragile Wood hite are found. In the extreme Arctic there are also species at are found nowhere else: beautiful Clouded Yellows, eenish with pink edging, many species of Fritillary, and

species of *Oeneis* which are related to the Grayling butterfly. *Erebia* species, dark Satyrids with little eye spots and russet banding, which are familiar to anyone used to visiting the higher parts of central Europe, fly even in the snow, where they are not at all concealed. Indeed, one or two species of this huge family are found only in the Arctic.

In Britain there are in the region of 68 butterfly species, and this number includes some which are not resident and migrate into the country each summer. But some of these are at the extreme northern limits of their range and are not to be found further north than the Midlands. Scotland and Ireland have many fewer species of butterflies than England. But Ireland has some adapted forms, notably the Common Blue and Marsh Fritillary, which are quite different and really rather prettier than the typical forms. Scotland, with its high mountains, has two *Erebias*, the Scotch Argus and the Small Mountain Ringlet. This last species is found in a few other places in Europe, but Britain does not have any species that are unique to her, only local races such as the English Swallowtail subspecies *britannicus*.

In France and Germany, and further south, there are more new species to be found, especially in the mountainous areas, the Alps in particular. Quite apart from the several species which are only to be found in restricted Alpine regions, there are butterflies to be seen in such profusion in almost any Alpine meadow that it seems unreal. In Austria, Switzerland and Italy there are areas where the meadows are so full of flowers that the grass is hardly visible. These are seldom sprayed or cultivated in any way except for the annual cut for hay and there are always inaccessible edges that are never cut at all. Here butterflies are able to breed undisturbed in surroundings which must seem like paradise to them, and certainly do to us! Here you will find several species of Large Copper, Blues of many species, *Erebias*, Clouded Yellows, Whites, Skippers, Vanessids and many more besides. The best months for enjoying butterflies are July and August, and the more time you spend the more you realize just what a rich variety there is. Some of the rarer butterflies found in the Alps are found elsewhere only in the extreme Arctic region, as if the races were stranded when the land in between warmed up. A Fritillary, *Boloria napaea*, is one of these and another is the Skipper, *Pyrgus andromedae*. A good many of the *Erebia* species are found only in the Alps: they are an interesting group, some of which can be difficult to identify. Other species found only in the Alps include Fritillaries, a Large Heath and the Apollo, *Parnassius phoebis*.

The warmer climate of the Mediterranean shores brings a transition between the cooler-climate species of the Alps and the typical butterflies of North Africa and, to the east, Asia Minor. The Two-tailed Pasha, the only European *Charaxes*, has a unique distribution which follows almost the entire Mediter-ranean coastline, in a band only a mile or two wide reachi from Portugal to Greece (but only on the *west* coast of Ital and all along the North African coast. The larva of this *Chara jasius* feeds on the strawberry tree, *Arbutus unedo*. A love form of Brimstone, *Gonepteryx cleopatra*, which has pools orange on the forewings, and *Leptidea duponchelli*, a relat of the Wood White, are found only in the Mediterrane region, with one colony in the south of France and the r being confined to Greece and Bulgaria. There are several l well-known relatives of the Orange Tip, found only in Spain North Africa; these include *Euchloë tagis*, *E. petchi* and *Zeg eupheme*. It is from this region, and especially from Nor Africa, that the Clouded Yellows, Painted Ladies and R Admirals originate each year and they continue to bre throughout the winter in the warmer climate.

In the extreme east of Europe there is an overlapping species from Asia. Some, like *Colias balkanica*, *Colias er* (both Clouded Yellows) and the Brimstone, *Gonepter farinosa*, are only just included in Europe and are really m Asiatic. In this eastern area too are some interesting Papilionid which are not quite like Apollos in appearance yet do not lo like Swallowtails, *Allancastria cerisyi* and *Archon apollin* These feed on *Aristolochia* like the *Zerinthias* (which used to known as *Thais*) that are found also in this region as well further along the Mediterranean. *Pontia chloridice*, a relative the Bath White, and the Bath White itself are found here on border with Asia Minor, and a lovely little Orange Tip, *Anth charis gruneri* occurs almost throughout the Grecian mainla This is an area where butterflies may in parts be a little spar but include many local and interesting species.

Previous pages, left: The White Admiral, *Limenitis camilla*, is a Nymphalid but otherwise not closely related to the Red Admiral. It is not at all common in Britain and is found in small colonies only in old deciduous woods where the larval food plant, honeysuckle, grows. The caterpillar in autumn spins itself a tent in a small, tightly rolled leaf which is fixed to the stem with silk to stop it falling in winter. In this hibernaculum the larva remains until spring when it comes out and starts to feed again. The caterpillar is very curiously shaped and beautifully coloured when fully grown. The butterfly emerges in July and measures 5 cm to 6 cm across.

Previous pages, right: Hardly anyone can fail to recognize the beautiful Red Admiral, *Vanessa atalanta*. It is well known all over Britain and the Continent but few people realize that, like the Painted Lady, the Red Admiral originates mainly from Africa and the Mediterranean shores. Those found further north have

migrated as a rule, although in good summers a generation is produced locally as far north as Britain. In the autumn there is evidence that some migrate south again but any that remain are killed by the winter climate almost without exception. The larvae feed only on nettle and they live in little tents formed from individual leaves with the edges joined with silk, to protect them from predators.

Left: The Meadow Brown, *Maniola jurtina*, is undoubtedly one of the commonest butterflies in Britain and generally in Europe. From late June onwards Meadow Browns are found very abundantly in almost any meadow or grassy hillside, and are often driven up almost in clouds as you walk through the long grass. The male, which is up to 4 cm across, is dark brown all over, with small eye spots on the forewing but the female is larger as a rule and has lovely orange-brown bands across the wings which, in certain geographical forms, can be greatly accentuated. The Meadow

Brown flies in a very unhurried way, stopping at almost every opportunity to feed from nearby flowers. Its eggs are laid on the grasses, which are the food plant of the caterpillar, and the green pupa is formed hanging by the tail amongst dense grass.

Above: The Duke of Burgundy Fritillary is the sole representative of the *Nemeobiidae* family in Europe and is closely related to the very large family of South American Erycinidae. This butterfly, *Hamearis lucina*, is not really a Fritillary at all but its colouring and pattern give it this appearance. *Hamearis* lives in grassy meadows and on hillsides where its food plants, cowslip and primrose, grow but in Britain it is localized and not found everywhere. The larva is pale translucent grey with black spotting and the pupa has just the same colouring and markings. It pupates in summer and the butterfly, which measures only about 2.5 cm across, emerges the following April and May.

Left: Although a black and white species the Marbled White, *Melanargia galathea* one of the Browns or Satyrids. It is a species which especially likes chalk downland or areas where the plant life i similar to that of chalk downs. In Britai the Marbled White is found mainly in th south but on the Continent it is a widespread species and in certain areas quite the commonest butterfly to be found. No other British species resembl it but there are a few closely allied spec on the Continent which could be confused with the Marbled White. The butterfly varies in size from 4 cm to 6 c across and there is tremendous variatior in colouring. Some are definitely yellow instead of white and on the underside o some forms the markings are yellowish brown instead of black.

Below: There is an enormous group of Fritillary butterflies in Europe, of which this *Melitaea didyma* is one of the most charming, not just for its looks but its 'friendliness'. You need only have a few of them in a breeding cage to find how they come and settle on your hand or arm and either sit there still or wheel about in tight circles. This is a species n found in Britain but common in parts o Central Europe. The larvae feed on plantain and can easily be raised in captivity. In size the butterflies vary fro 3 cm to 5 cm; they are closely allied to the Marsh Fritillary.

Right: The likeness to a lucerne leaf of the Green Hairstreak, *Callophrys rubi*, i this picture is coincidental, as it has no special relationship with the plant, but it shows just how well concealed it is when at rest. It is the only all-green butterfly in Europe. Rather less than 2 cm across, the Green Hairstreak is not uncommon either in Britain or Europe and is found most frequently on chalky hills or heathland where its larval food plants, rock rose, gorse and dogwood usually grow. The upperside is a uniform chocolate brown with a velvety texture.

Left: One of the few butterflies that is extending its range in Britain is the Comma butterfly, *Polygonia c-album*, pictured here. Once a rarity except in th south it is now spreading through the Midlands. In Europe it is widespread an quite often met with on the edges of woodland and in gardens and orchards where it likes to feed, especially in the autumn from fallen fruit. The irregular wingshape is a characteristic of the genu *Polygonia* and the names Comma and *c-album* come from the white C or commalike marking on the underside of the hindwing.

Centre: The Orange Tip, *Anthocharis cardamines*, is one of the most beautiful and delicate of all British and European butterflies, although only the male has the bright orange tips to the forewings. In May, the butterflies emerge from the pupae, and they are around 4 cm across and the eggs are laid on garlic mustard and cuckoo flower especially. If two egg are laid on one stem, one of the resulting caterpillars will eat the other, thus making sure there will be enough for it to eat on the very slender food plant. The pupa is particularly unusual, being very angular and easily mistaken for a thorn or seed pod when attached to a twig for the winter.

Below: When the Orange Tip rests on it food plant, garlic mustard, it is so like t flowers that it is almost impossible to se The underside hindwing is apparently so patterned with green that the camouflag is almost perfect: the green effect, however, in fact results from tiny scales of black and yellow which give the illusion of green. This is almost unbelievable until seen under the microscope. The caterpillars are also masters of deception with counter shading which makes them seem to merg into the thin stem on which they feed.

Top right: The Large Blue butterfly, *Maculinea arion*, has amongst British butterflies, a completely unique life cycle. The butterfly (about 4 cm across) lays its eggs singly on the flowers of wild thyme, upon which the newly hatched caterpillar will feed for the first three weeks of its life. After this it changes its skin and in its third instar drops onto the ground and wanders off. It now depends for life on being found by an ant (of the genus *Myrmica* only) which will take it off to the ants' nest. Here it lives amongst the ant brood and is fed as if part of the family. It hibernates there and in the spring starts to grow rapidly, devouring the ant brood, until it pupates in the nest in Jur The butterfly emerges in July by scrabbling through a narrow tunnel to the surface. The Large Blue, though found on the Continent (where it lays it eggs on marjoram as well as thyme), is now in great danger of extinction in

Britain and is only found in a few tiny colonies in southwest England.

Right: Still found in quite large colonies on almost every grassy hill or meadow is the Common Blue, *Polyommatus icarus*. As with most other Blues, the females of the Common Blue are mostly brown and quite unlike the males except for the underside wing pattern. The Common Blue measures 2 cm to 3 cm across: it is greatly subject to variation of the underside wing pattern and the females have varying amounts of blue on the upper side. A beautiful form from Ireland has a great deal of blue and orange, while others are quite drab and brown. The larvae feed on bird's-foot trefoil and are very often attended by ants for the honeydew that they secrete from a gland near the tail.

Left: In flight the Green-veined White, *Pieris napi*, is hard to distinguish from the Cabbage Whites, especially the Small White, but when it rests on a flower the strong veining can be seen, especially on the underside where the veins are greenish and very bold. This species is not a pest of cabbages and breeds naturally on wild horseradish, garlic mustard and other wild Cruciferae. The pupal stage lasts the winter and the butterflies are some of the first to emerge in spring. The butterfly measures about 5 cm across, and is subject to colour variation.

Below: In Britain the Pale Clouded Yellow, *Colias hyale*, is greatly valued as an extremely rare migrant but over most of the Continent this species is a lot commoner than the brighter orange Clouded Yellow which visits Britain by migration each summer. Their abundance depends each year almost entirely on the climate and current weather conditions. Neither *Colias* species can survive the British winter. The larvae feed on clove and other leguminous plants; they are continuously brooded and in captivity will produce a brood at Christmas time These species originate from Africa and the Mediterranean region and migrate north each spring and summer. Their wingspan is around 5 cm.

Right: The leaflike appearance of the Brimstone, *Gonepteryx rhamni*, helps t protect it while it is hibernating, hidde usually amongst evergreens such as ivy. You will very rarely see the Brimstone resting with its wings open, exposing the beautiful deep yellow upperside; it sits with its wings closed as in the photograph. Only the male has the brig yellow colour and the female is a very pale eau-de-nil. Brimstones can be seen flying as early as February if the weath is fine, but they do not start breeding until later when the leaves of their food plant, buckthorn, start to open. Brimstones measure about 6 cm across.

Left: One of the largest butterflies in
Europe is the Swallowtail, *Papilio
machaon*, which measures up to 8 cm or
9 cm across. There are geographical race
in many parts of the world but the best
known are the very rare English race fro
Norfolk, known as *britannicus*, and the
Continental *P.m. gorganus*. *Britannicus* i
darker and lives in remote parts of the
Norfolk Broads on the marsh plant,
milk parsley; the Continental race is
paler and prefers drier mountainous are
where it feeds on many related
Umbelliferae, including garden carrot.
The Swallowtail can be bred in captivity
fairly easily and has very beautiful green
larvae striped with orange and black.

Below: In Britain the Scarce Swallowtai
Iphiclides podalirius, has been recorded
only as an occasional migrant but there
are parts of the Continent where it is
frequently seen. Its favourite haunts are
woodlands and hedgerows, and above al
orchards where the larvae can feed on
plum and pear trees. Its wild food plant
blackthorn. The Scarce Swallowtail vari
from 6 cm to 9 cm across. The butterfly
emerges in May after spending the winte
as a pupa and in warmer climates a
second brood is produced in the late
summer. In captivity *I. podalirius* is not
easy to breed but if larvae are obtained
they can be raised quite easily.

European butterflies
1 *Pieris brassicae*, the Large White
2 *Inachis io*, the Peacock 3 *Argynnis
paphia*, the Silver-washed Fritillary
4 *Melageria daphnis* 5 *Carterocephalu
palaemon*, the Chequered Skipper, now
great rarity in Britain 6 *Ochlodes
venata*, the Large Skipper
7 *Scolitantides orion* 8 *Thymelicus
sylvestris*, the Small Skipper 9 *Heode*
virgaureae, the Fiery Copper
10 *Issionia lathonia*, the Queen of Spain
Fritillary, a very rare migrant to Britain
(found throughout Europe, however, no
only in Spain) 11 *Parnassius apollo*,
the mountain Apollo butterfly
12 *Euphydryas maturna*, the Scarce
Fritillary (related to the Marsh
Fritillary) 13 *Lycaena dispar*, the
famous Large Copper, extinct in Britain
since 1843 14 *Clossiana euphrosyne*,
the Pearl-bordered Fritillary 15 *Erebi*
ligea, the Arran Brown found principally
in the Alps but also in the Arctic
16 *Vanessa polychloros*, the Large
Tortoiseshell, now a great rarity in
Britain 17 *Aglais urticae*, the Small
Tortoiseshell 18 *Apatura iris*, the
Purple Emperor 19 *Pararge megera*,
the Wall Brown 20 *Vanessa cardui*,
the Painted Lady

These butterflies are all life size.

African Butterflies

The region being considered here extends from South Africa northwards to the northern limits of the Sahara Desert, and includes Egypt. The Sahara forms an effective barrier between the African faunistic region and the European or Palearctic region. Very few insects cross the desert and in any case the climate north of the Sahara is that of the Mediterranean with a prolonged cool period in winter. The Atlas Mountains, which stretch across Algeria and Morocco into Tunisia, have a very cold winter with snow blocking the passes for six to eight months of the year, while south of the Sahara there is tropical rain forest with no true winter and vegetation that continues its growth throughout the year. Therefore the northern part of Africa has been considered as being in the European region.

An interesting aspect of African vegetation, which has a great bearing on its insect population, is the fact that there is hardly a plant growing wild in Africa which does not scratch, sting, pierce or hook into the clothing of the passing traveller. So many of the trees found there, like the common acacias and mimosas, have branches covered with prickly thorns, which even drop off and cover the ground to catch in your feet. This is because the present flora of Africa is only a small remnant of a once enormous number of species of plants from which all the un-thorny, edible and leafy plants and trees have been gradually exterminated by the phenomenal abundance in Africa of vegetarian animals. Herd after herd of animals, which were once much commoner than they are today, would pass through region, stripping it of everything green until the prickly and unpalatable species were the only ones left able to propagate themselves and the unprotected plants began to die out. As a result, there is an almost complete absence of insects that are limited to feeding only on one plant, because they have adapted to be able to accept a wide range of food plants. This is a great help to the butterfly breeder who is trying to raise African butterflies in a temperate climate.

The character of the terrain of a continent affects butterflies and their habits very directly. In a country where high mountains create cut-off pockets, as in the Asiatic Himalayas, new forms and species have developed, but in Africa there are almost no continental divisions, which has resulted in a universal distribution of species with very few being found in one particular small area. A prime example of this is *Papilio demodocus*, which is found equally commonly all over Africa, except for some reason in Egypt. Save for certain forest species this is true of many other butterflies also. Another interesting characteristic of African butterflies is their adaptation to the dry dusty conditions and their matching colours of reddish brown, greys and red-yellows. Barely a third of African butterflies are not coloured red-brown and this colour is found in almost all Acraeas, Danaids, *Precis*, many *Charaxes* and *Cymothoë*.

In Africa there are more than 1500 species of butterflies, many of which are only found on this continent. Two outstanding

g species that come to mind are *Papilio antimachus* and
Papilio zalmoxis which, although not Birdwings, can be con-
dered as being in the same class as those East Indian giants.
Papilio antimachus, a species with a wingspan of 20 to 25 cm, is
the largest African butterfly. It has very narrow wings patterned
with red-brown and looks like a giant Acraea. This magnificent
butterfly lives in the rain forest of central Africa and the female
is so rare that probably fewer than 10 have ever been caught or
even seen. Nobody knows anything of the life history or the
food plant of *P. antimachus*. The same applies with the female
of the other giant species, *Papilio zalmoxis*. *P. zalmoxis* has a
pure yellow body like the Birdwings and the wings are steely
blue, rayed with black. The *Papilios* include a small number of
attractive species such as the black and yellow *demodocus*,
phidicephalus and *dardanus*, and a group of black Swallowtails
banded with iridescent blue-green, the nireus group. Rarer
species like *P. nobilis* and *rex* are always looked for by collectors but there is a large number of *Papilio* species, many very
rare indeed, which are not dull, precisely, but are patterned only
with black and white or brown and white. The natural and
geographical variation is one of the most interesting attractions
that African *Papilios* hold for collectors.

Amongst the Pieridae there are no large species comparable
with the Giant Orange Tip of Asia or the very large Brimstones
of America. Many are about the same size and shape as the
European Cabbage Whites but infinitely variable and often very
colourful. *Mylothris* is a genus of colourful butterflies but the
largest of all and the most spectacular is the genus *Colotis*,
all of which have brilliantly coloured tips to the forewings.
Few *Colotis* occur outside Africa and this group is therefore
one of Africa's greatest butterfly assets.

Danaids are very common but there are relatively few
species, many of which are mimicked by other butterflies. There
are no *Euploea* in Africa. A genus that is only found there,
however, is *Amauris,* mostly large, black-and-white species
which are mimicked by *Papilio dardanus* females. Few of the
Satyridae are outstanding among the world's butterflies and
most are quite small, except for *Melanitis*, the Evening Brown
which is also found in Asia. The *Elymniopsis* is interesting for
its similarity to the palm flies, *Elymnias*, found in Asia. One
very striking butterfly, a very local and restricted species from
South Africa, is the Table Mountain Brown, *tullbaghia*, with a
wingspan of 10 cm.

African Nymphalidae, relatives of the Peacocks and Fritillaries of Europe, are very numerous and include many very
colourful species that are only found in Africa. The *Charaxes*,
large and very robust butterflies capable of tremendous speeds,
are one group that immediately comes to mind. They have
intricately patterned under sides and nearly all the species are
beautiful. Collectors obtain *Charaxes* by trapping with bait in
netting traps as they are not easy to find without bait. Some
Charaxes are very rare. *Cymothoë* is an important genus and
includes the blood-red *sangaris*. *Euphaedra* are seldom well
represented in collections but these are quite numerous and
include species with lovely markings in unusual shades of green
and orange with areas of magenta. *Hypolimnas* are important in
Africa because of their incredible mimetic forms. The Mother-
of-Pearl butterflies, *Salamis*, are outstanding and there is a
group of the Pansy butterflies, *Precis*, which is much larger than
in any other part of the world.

The Acraeas are sometimes treated as a family on their own. They are almost exclusively African and very numerous. They are mostly medium-sized, slightly transparent species and a few are exceptionally beautiful. They are poisonous to birds and use very involved mimicry. *Planema* is a large, closely allied genus.

The Lycaenidae, the Blues, Coppers and Hairstreaks, constitute one third of all African butterflies. Some are among the world's most attractive butterflies but are seldom seen in collections. *Epitola*, a brilliant blue species, quite unlike a Lycaenid is equal to anything found in South America.

In Africa you find some of the most striking examples of mimicry. Batesian mimicry, when a butterfly mimics the pattern of another that is distasteful to birds, is found amongst *Hypolimnas*, which take on almost the precise colouring and marking of *Lymnas* and *Amauris*, both species that are decidedly poisonous. The females of *Papilio dardanus*, but not the males, are found in numerous mimetic forms, with further examples found amongst the Lycaenidae (particularly *Pentila* and *Pseudacraea*. But there are also examples of distasteful butterflies, which are already protected by being poisonous mimicking the coloration and pattern of other distasteful species. This is known as Müllerian mimicry, and it is not as pointless as may at first seem. If two similar-looking distasteful species exist in one area, the two species combined will only have to sacrifice a certain number of butterflies before birds recognize them as being distasteful and this number is precisely half what it would have been if the two species had existed in differing colour forms.

Previous pages, left: *Papilio demodocus*, the Citrus Swallowtail, is probably Africa's commonest Swallowtail. It is known also as the Christmas butterfly, because it is particularly abundant at that time of the year. *P. demodocus* measures some 10 cm across and its large caterpillar can be quite a pest in citrus orchards. The caterpillar is very striking with a disruptive patterning of grey on green and prominent and frightening eyelike markings up near the head.

Previous pages, right: There is no other butterfly in the world that matches the blood-red of the beautiful *Cymothoë sangaris*. In the same genus are some other beautiful orange-red species and this bright colouring is found only in the males, the females being duller, marked with wavy lines and often bearing little or no red. Reds are relatively uncommon in butterflies and are found in spots and patches rather than all over the wings as in *C. sangaris*. It is a butterfly of the forest regions, found especially in central Africa where it occurs in considerable numbers. *Sangaris* is small, with a wingspan of barely 5 cm.

Above: One of the Pieridae, *Eronia cleodora* is a very common butterfly in South Africa to Abyssinia. In the summer it occurs as a very much larger and brighter form, often found flying in groups, possibly with migratory tendencies. The upperside is much plainer, being a pale yellow with broad dark borders. *Cleodora* inhabits dry scrub but is found quite generally, including in gardens. The larva, which feeds on species of the shrub *Capparis*, is green with a bright reddish-yellow line along the side. The butterfly varies in wingspan from 5 cm to 7 cm.

Right: The tropical Skipper butterflies are an amazing sight to anyone who is only familiar with the Skippers found in Europe. The European Skippers average 1.5 cm to 2 cm across but this giant species, *Leucochitonea levubu* from Africa is a good 5 cm in wingspan, and some species come even larger. The Skippers have so many individual characteristics that it has been proposed that they should be considered as a group on their own, neither as butterflies nor as moths. They have a characteristic way of sunning themselves with their hindwings held flat and level, protruding in front of the forewings which are held in an almost vertical plane. No other group could be confused with the Skippers when this position is seen.

Left: *Charaxes jasius saturnus*. The *Charaxes* butterflies are one of the principal groups found in Africa, which is their main stronghold. They are robu very fast-flying Nymphalids which are often attracted to flowers but prefer tr sap, other sweet liquids and fruit as we as less savoury dung and carrion. They are easily attracted to bait and collecto usually obtain them with specially constructed netting traps baited with fruit. *C. jasius* is found also in Europe, the only *Charaxes* that is, but the subspecies *saturnus* is solely African an is one of the prettiest of all the *Charax*

Below left: This is one of the Kite Swallowtails which are found in all tropical regions. Its rather triangular shape is reminiscent of a kite, but although they are called Swallowtails, all species, like this *Papilio pylades*, in fact have tails. *Pylades* measures about 6 cm across. It is not one of the prolific African Swallowtails, but it is widespre being found from Natal in the south right up to the northern Congo.
The form illustrated is called *angolanus* and actually comes from Kenya. It was photographed immediately after emergence and its wings have only just dried. The pupa has a curious pointed projection 5 or 6 mm long on the thora which is found on most Kite Swallow-tail pupae. The larva feeds on citrus.

Top right: *Lymnas chrysippus* form *alcippus*. This form of *L. chrysippus*, th Plain Tiger, differs in having almost all-white hindwings. It usually flies amongst the typical form but is found most commonly in the West African rai forest where it almost completely supersedes the typical form which has orange hindwings. Both forms are not only distasteful to birds but decidedly poisonous, sufficient to kill even a smal mammal. Predators learn to recognize t colours and patterns and avoid those w warning coloration. The poisons in *L. chrysippus* are derived from the cater-pillar's food plants, which are various s of poisonous *Asclepias* or milkweeds. T butterflies are very variable in size, ranging from 6 cm to 9 cm across.

Right: *Acraea encedon* form *alcippina*. The appearance and name of this butterfly quickly shows a remarkable resemblance to form *alcippus* of the Plain Tiger. This is a prime example of mimicry, by which a butterfly escapes predation by taking on the warning colours of a butterfly that is recognized by predators as being distasteful or poisonous. When *encedon alcippina* is flying even the most experienced observer can hardly detect the differenc between the two species and certainly a bird could be expected to confuse the two. Furthermore, this remarkable butterfly also mimics the several other quite distinct forms of the Plain Tiger, producing the colour form that matche the model of its own particular locality

Left: The Red Tips and Purple Tips of Africa are some of the most charming butterflies of that continent. The genus *Colotis* (known as *Teracolus* in many works) is very large and varied. The majority are white with the tips red (like the *Colotis antevippe* illustrated) but some have the most magnificent iridescent purple, shown here in *Colotis ione*, and there are also species with a lemon-yellow ground colour. Not only are all of these normally variable but each also produces quite distinctly different forms in the wet and dry seasons, which makes identification of the *Colotis* quite difficult. Most *Colotis* are common and fly throughout the year.

Below: The group of butterflies known as the Pansy butterflies (*Precis* species) is very well represented in Africa, and one of the loveliest is this *Precis westermanni*. It is a medium-sized species, with a 5 cm wingspan, and distinct from the other Pansies in its bright and clearly defined markings, but the female is not as bright and is quite differently marked from the male illustrated here. *P. westermanni* is found mainly in East Africa, where it is widespread though not one of the most abundant of the *Precis* species.

Top right: Africa is rich in the Lycaenidae, which include some of the most beautiful, jewel-like butterflies in the world. This Hairstreak butterfly, *Myrina silenus*, is little more than 3 cm across. It is exquisitely coloured and has very robust tails, which are curled so that the pale underside colour shows at the tips when at rest. The caterpillar is green, decorated with white tubercles. It feeds on species of *Ficus* (which includes figs) and is often found closely attended by numbers of ants: these are attracted by a gland near the tail which secretes a sweet substance that the ants like to drink.

Right: The incredibly long feathery tails of this butterfly are characteristic of the genus *Hypolycaena*; this particular species is *H. antijanus*. The wingspan is about 3 cm and the hindwing with the tails is quite as long again as this. Only tropical Lycaenids have these very long and elaborate tails, yet surprisingly they are capable of fairly rapid flight, though this is not usually sustained. The butterfly is constantly stopping to rest on a leaf and can be seen 'cleaning its whiskers' and antennae with its forelegs, just like a little animal. The eggs and larvae of *antijanus* are so similar to those of others in the genus that identification can only be verified when the actual butterfly emerges.

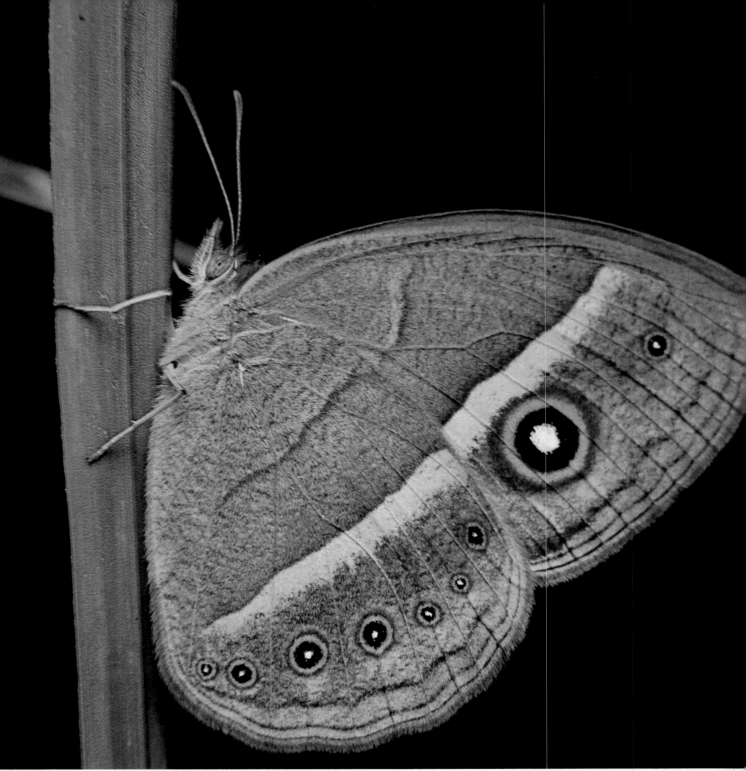

Above: *Henotesia perspicua*. The Marsh
Butterfly is a grass-feeding Satyrid which
might well be confused with *Mycalesis*
but is distinguished by the fact that it
has densely hairy eyes. On the wings the
little eye spots draw the attention of
predators which naturally attack the eyes,
but this results only in wing damage and
the butterfly escapes death. This is a form
of protection which is adopted
particularly by the Satyridae. Little is
known of the early stages of *Henotesia*'s
life cycle and on the continent of Africa
only a few species occur, but there are
many species in Madagascar which
are only found on that island.

African butterflies
1 *Salamis aethiops*, the Mother-of-Pearl
butterfly   2 *Hypolimnas dexithea*,
which is found only in Madagascar
3 *Precis octavia*, a curious butterfly which
looks like this in the wet season and in
the dry season appears in the blue form
sesamus, illustrated as No 4   5 *Epitola
posthumus*, a giant Lycaenid found only
in Africa   6 *Charaxes eupale*, small for
a *Charaxes* and unusually coloured
7 *Charaxes pollux*, a typical *Charaxes*
8 An *Acraea* species, one of a large group
of distasteful species, often very common,
some of which are extremely pretty
9 *Aphnaeus*, one of the world's

loveliest Hairstreaks, seen from the under
side, and in No 10 from the upperside
11 A *Colotis* species, a Pierid found
mainly in Africa which is subject to
seasonal variation. This dark form is the
wet season form   12 *Papilio (Druria)
antimachus*, a unique species (whose
female is one of the rarest butterflies in
the world)   13 *Lepidochrysops
giganthea*, an uncommon African
Lycaenid

North American Butterflies

The Nearctic region covers Alaska and the Arctic zone and stretches southwards through the temperate zones of Canada and the United States to the subtropical climate of Florida and Mexico. In this southern area there is an overlapping of butterflies from Central American countries and some quite exotic species are found that more truly form part of the fauna of countries as far south as Brazil. Nymphalids such as *Chlorippe*, the leaflike *Anaea* species with its varied and exotic colour, *Dione* (the Gulf Fritillary) the long-tailed *Megalura*, and even *Callicore*, which with *Catagramma* are very much considered as being South American species. One Swallowtail also merges into the North American or Nearctic region from the tropical south, *Papilio thoas,* a very large brown-and-yellow banded species with long tails, a visitor to citrus orchards where the larvae feed.

Although almost all the species have some differences distinguishing them from those found in Europe, there is a great overall resemblance between the two butterfly fauna, and an equally close relationship. This could be accounted for by the fact that the two continents cover a similar range of climate

nd latitudes; or, possibly, that, in the course of evolution, the
eparation of the two continents by the Atlantic Ocean has led
o a subtle diversification of species from common ancestors.
he same thing is noticeable between some of the butterflies
ound in, for instance, Tasmania and those in Europe. In
asmania, there are butterflies on heathland which are in the
ame family as the Wall Browns, Blues and Vanessids that you
ould find in Europe and their resemblance to these is strik-
ngly similar, yet they are different species which are found only
n the southern hemisphere. Nor is this comparison seen only in
he butterflies; it is visible in the plants too. One example is a
lant that grows like and looks like heather — but isn't heather.
he study of North American butterflies, therefore, can enable
s to draw comparisons with their European counterparts, and
elp a great deal in the understanding of comparative evolution.

The American Arctic region has a wider range of butterflies
an that found in the European Arctic. One of the loveliest
pecies is one of the Apollos, *Parnassius eversmanni*, a rather
re species whose male, unique among *Parnassius*, is lemon
yellow with the usual contrasting markings of this tribe in red
and black. This particular species occurs in Siberia too, and as
an extreme rarity on high mountains in Japan. The American
Arctic also has a green species of *Colias*, a number of *Oeneis*, the
Grayling-like Satyrids (this is really their headquarters) and a
whole host of Fritillaries which make very interesting study.

In fact it is on this continent that the world's Fritillaries are
most highly developed and all over the United States there are
dozens of species, most of which are not found outside
America. A very outstanding species, especially for a temperate
region, is the giant *Argynnis diana*, whose wingspan in both
sexes is over 10 cm. The male has a large central black area, with
a broad border of typical Fritillary red-brown or orange, but the
female, unlike any other Fritillary in the world, is blue and
black. This is a very local species found only in parts of
California. Other large species that are unusual include *Argynnis
idalia*, with prominent under side spotting in silver, and *A.
nokomis*, but there are more than a score of other large
Argynnis and *Speyeria*. *Boloria*, relatives of the Pearl-bordered

Fritillaries, are well represented, especially in the Arctic, and the *Melitaea* species or Chequer Spots which are related to the European Marsh Fritillary also appear in force. In addition to all these there is a genus of small Fritillaries not found outside America, known as *Phycoides*, and these are numerous.

America has no less than 10 *Polygonia* species, close relations of the European Comma. One has the confusing name of *Comma*, another, illustrated on page 36, is called the Question Mark and has the Latin name *P. interrogationis*. The other Vanessids are represented by milberti, which looks like a superb variety of the Small Tortoiseshell, the Painted Lady (there is no continent where this species does not appear) and the Hunter's Painted Lady, known as a rare migrant to Europe, the Mourning Cloak, and one or two others. But there is no Peacock nor anything resembling it. There are at least six *Limenitis* species, related to the White Admiral, and one of these is the famous *archippus* which mimics the Monarch butterfly (both are illustrated on the previous pages).

Satyrids, the Browns, are very varied and interesting. They include the Heaths, *Coenonympha*, some *Erebias*, *Neonympha* (in America only), some very handsome *Satyrus* species and the Arctic *Oeneis*. Skippers or Hesperiidae are numerous and include giant species, some with long curved tails almost like miniature Swallowtails.

The Lycaenids include no fewer than 40 species of Hairstreaks. As in Europe they are mostly smaller species but they are colourful and there are one or two exceptionally beautiful and large ones such as *halesus* and *chrysalus*. There are at least 13 Coppers, but they do not compare in brilliance with those found in Europe. The Blues are very numerous and attractive: one pretty little species unlike any other in the world is *Lycaena*

sonorensis, which is blue with four orange splotches, one o each wing, as if it had been haphazardly daubed with a pain brush.

Amongst the Pierids America has some real gems. The *Colia* like Dog Face butterflies are unique, and the true *Colias* a more numerous here than in Europe. There are some ve attractive rare *Colias*, especially in the Arctic. The Orange Tip *Anthocharis*, are not common but there are some attracti species. *A. sara* is widespread and occurs in many forms. Tl prettiest of all, *Anthocharis pima*, is illustrated on page 3 There are several *Catopsilia*, of which *C. philea* is one of tl finest in the world. Here too are *Eurema* species, similar those found in the tropics, but some of the American speci excel all others in size, shape and richness of colour, especiall the pure orange species *E. nicippe* and *proterpia*.

American *Papilios* are particularly interesting to the speciali and many of them are both large and attractive. There is a grou of Tiger Swallowtails which are slightly kite-shaped and beau fully tailed, yellow with bars of black. The better-known ones this group are *P. glaucus* and *rutulus*. *P. ajax* is a true Kite Swordtail butterfly; it is a rather 'local' species, not at all wid spread. One *Aristolochia*-feeding Swallowtail is American, tl Pipe Vine Swallowtail, *P. philenor*. *P. cresphontes* is a Nor American species very similar to *P. thoas* of the south: it found in citrus orchards. In addition to these species and couple of others not mentioned, there is an important grou related to *P. machaon*. There are seven of these, includi *polyxenes asterias* and *zelicaon* (illustrated), and some very da species, the finest of which is *brevicauda*, which is difficult find. *Papilio machaon* itself is entirely an Arctic species America and is given the subspecific name of *aliaska*.

evious pages, left: This butterfly is one f the most famous in the world. In orth America it is known as the onarch, in England as the Milkweed, d in Australia as the Wanderer, or to eryone as *Danaus plexippus*. It has wingspan that can measure up to 12 cm d is a powerful flier and can actually fly ght across the Atlantic from America the shores of Britain, where it is und as a very rare migrant. In Europe breeds in the Canary Isles but its range restricted to places where its nonhardy od plants, the milkweeds, grow. These ntain a poison that renders *plexippus* noxious to would-be predators. The terpillar is beautifully patterned in ack and yellow warning colours and e pupa is a translucent green, jewelled ith silver and gold. If the food plant is own, *plexippus* is quite possible to ar in captivity.

evious pages, right: *Limenitis archippus*, e North American Viceroy, has a ttern so similar to that of the Monarch at it escapes predation even though it neither poisonous or distasteful. The iceroy in fact comes from the ymphalid family and is more closely lated to the White Admirals than to the onarch. It is considerably smaller, proximately 7 cm across, but this is ot unusual between a model and a mimic d birds are still deceived despite the ze difference. The caterpillar is curiously imped, much like the other White dmirals, and feeds on willow. The iceroy is well distributed over ost of the United States.

Previous pages, bottom right: The Arctic has a substantial and very interesting butterfly fauna, especially in the Nearctic or American sector. This is one of the *Oeneis* species which have quite a resemblance to the European Grayling butterflies and are, in fact, closely related to them. In size they range from 4 cm to 6 cm across and there are more than a dozen species, all of which are found only in the Arctic or at the summits of exceptionally high mountains. There are European *Oeneis* too, both in the Arctic and in the highest Alps. The larvae are tapered at the head and tail and look much like other Satyrid larvae: they are all grass-feeders and are able to withstand temperatures well below zero, even down to minus 21° Centigrade. This butterfly from the Yukon is *Oeneis jutta*.

Left: The Mourning Cloak, *Nymphalis antiopa*, derives its name from the appearance of the dark central area of the wings, which looks like a black funeral cloak, with the fringe of the more light-hearted dress showing beneath. In England this butterfly is known as the Camberwell Beauty, because it was in this part of London that it was first discovered, on top of an open horse-drawn bus. It is a butterfly greatly prized by collectors in Britain as a very rare migrant from European countries where it breeds and is relatively common, as it is also in North America under its other name. The Mourning Cloak breeds in woodlands and the butterflies feed from tree sap and fruit as well as nectar.

Top left: Looking at the pattern on the forewings of this butterfly it is easy to see why it has been named Dog Face — the resemblance to the head of a poodle is quite striking. This species is *Meganostoma caesonia* from North America and there is only one other in the same genus: *M. eurydice*, also North American. Both look very much like *Colias*, and they are in fact closely related. The larvae feed on leguminous plants such as clovers and trefoils. Both the male and female of *caesonia* are similarly marked though distinguishable, yet the female of *eurydice* could easily be mistaken for a Brimstone.

Top right: A very splendid butterfly is this North American Tiger Swallowtail *Papilio glaucus*. In the north specimens can measure around 10 cm across and they become larger the further south you go, until in the extreme south there are giants up to 16 cm across. About 50 per cent of the females that emerge resemble the males in colouring but the remainder are so different as to be mistaken for quite another species, especially *Papilio troilus*. *Glaucus* is attracted to puddles and damp places, carrion and manure, and it has even been reported to be attracted by tobacco smoke. The larva, which has very prominent eye spots feeds on wild cherry, ash, lime, birch and tulip tree. It lives in one-leaf tents which it makes by drawing the sides of the leaf together and binding them with silk. The Tiger Swallowtail is reasonably common and widespread in the United States but is seldom found in abundance in any one place.

Top: Closely related to the European Comma is this North American species called the Question Mark, *Polygonia interrogationis*. The names are derived from small, clearly-defined white markings on the underside hindwing which bear a resemblance to these punctuation marks. The *Polygonias* all have the same curiously tattered edge to the wings which at first sight looks li[ke] damage but is in fact extremely beautiful and almost unique in the butterfly world. Freshly emerged Question Marks have a lovely plum-coloured bloom all over the wings. They are widely dispersed and quite common

ft: The Hickory Hairstreak (*Strymon ryaevorus*) is a recently discovered ecies in North America, which is very re and certainly local. It is a species und only in the most northerly states d in a part of Canada, and flies only ring the month of July. As yet the terpillar and other early stages of its e are barely known but it breeds on ckory. The wingspan is 3 cm, not as ge as most of the American Hairstreaks.

ntre: This beautiful Orange Tip tterfly must be one of the loveliest in e world. It is one of quite a large family American Orange Tips but only this,

Anthocharis pima, has such a brilliant yellow ground colour. The red on the upperside tips is also on the underside and the hindwings are heavily marked with solid green bands. *Pima* is, unfortunately, very uncommon and appears to be restricted to Arizona. The larva undoubtedly would feed on one of the Cruciferae but the early stages and complete life history appear to be unknown. The wingspan is under 4 cm.

Above: Shown here is the American Black Swallowtail, *Papilio polyxenes asterias*. It is closely related to the European Swallowtail, *P. machaon*, and

except that it is much blacker the markings are very similar and the two species will interbreed successfully, producing progeny that are extremely variable in intensity of markings. The caterpillar is green, striped with black and orange — warning colours, so although this is not a poisonous species it is able to deceive predators. The Black Swallowtail hibernates in the pupal stage, with the pupa held securely to a twig by a silken girdle, until its emergence, usually in May. It is widespread and often found in gardens where it lays its eggs on carrot leaves; in wild places it chooses other species of *Umbelliferae*.

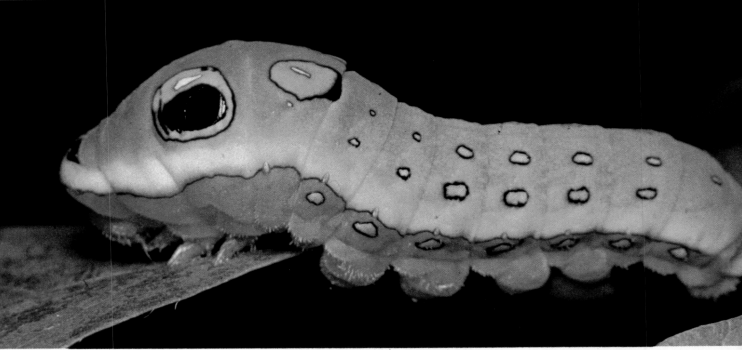

Top: North America has a number of *Papilio* species which bear a strong resemblance to the European *P. machaon* and this *P. zelicaon* is probably the closest of all. It is found as far north as Vancouver Island and all the way south to Arizona. The life history is similar to that of the other *machaon* and the larvae, which can be distinguished from those of *machaon* by their much paler green colour, likewise feed on Umbelliferae.

Above: The caterpillar of the Spicebush Swallowtail, *Papilio troilus*, has markings which not only make it look attractive but also help to protect it from predators, which are wary of its eye spots. A number of *Papilio* larvae in the tropics have these markings but few species look quite the same. This caterpillar feeds on spicebush,

sassafras and other plants mostly found only in America. The butterfly emerges early, usually in April and May, and there are two broods, with a third in the warmer south. It is found particularly in shady woods but is also seen in fields and gardens, visiting flowers and sailing close to the ground with a slow flight which distinguishes it from some of the *machaon*-like Swallowtails.

North American butterflies

1 *Catopsilia philea*, a large species found in the extreme south   2 *Argynnis diana* is the largest temperate zone Fritillary: the female is larger than the male and coloured blue and black instead of the normal orange and black   3 *Colias behri*, a rare Arctic Clouded Yellow   4 *Precis lavinia*, which is common in America and can easily be raised on plantain   5 *Papilio*

(Battus) philenor, the Pipe Vine Swallowtail   6 *Aglais milberti*, a close relative of the Small Tortoiseshell   7 The *Dismorphia* extend just into the southern States: note the curious wing shape of this Pierid   8 A Dog Face butterfly, *Meganastoma eurydice*   9 *Euphydryas phaeton*, an American Marsh Fritillary   10 Almost extinct, and for years thought to be so, is this *Papilio aristodemus ponceanus*, which was recently rediscovered in Florida   11 Hunter's Painted Lady, *Vanessa virginiensis*, which is a very rare migrant to Britain   12 *Eurema nicippe*, a pretty orange species   13 *Parnassius smintheus* one of America's three *Parnassius* species   14 Another member of the *Eurema* genus which has an unusual wing shape, *E. gundlachia* comes from the extreme south of the continent.

South American Butterflies

Between the North American and South American continen
there is rather less overlapping of species than there is, f
instance, between Europe and Asia, where there is a merger
the butterflies from each of these two regions. There is only
narrow neck of land between the Americas and the presence
some tropical species in the southern United States seems to
rather an infiltration from the tropics farther south than a tru
overlapping of the two faunas. Certainly quite few essential
North American species are found south of Mexico.

South America has a richness of species that is unequalled.
remarkable number of the butterflies also have brilliant an
conspicuous colours. Because there are no pronounced rair
seasons, such as you find in Africa, there is no noticeab
seasonal variation in South American butterflies. Adaptations
local climates and habitats are also less noticeable in Sou
American butterflies than in those from Africa and Asia.

urious feature, for which there seems no obvious reason, is that n South America some species that are normally tailless, like ome Skippers, Erycinids and some of the Nymphalids, occur ith very pronounced tails.

Mimicry in South America is taken to great lengths by some pecialized groups, not only among butterflies but moths too. he moths mimic each other, they copy colourful and dreaded pecies of wasps, and they also copy butterflies. Thus South merica can offer you the incredible sight of a flowering shrub eing visited by four or five different kinds of butterfly or oth, all of which are wearing uniform colours and patterns. An xample of such a situation might be constituted of a Danaid, *ycorea*, which is orange-brown patterned with yellow and ack, a Pierid, *Perhybris*, with precisely the same colouring as model, *Dismorphia* (which is another Pierid), a Heliconiid d a moth, *Chetone*. The advantage to each species becomes

apparent when you consider how few individuals would have to be lost to predators before this warning pattern was recognized, compared with the result if each kind had a completely different colour. The same situation can occur with another group of unrelated species, which are black with a prominent bar of red.

It is necessary to pick out some of the most noteworthy South American butterflies for mention in this section, and the richness makes this peculiarly difficult. Some will inevitably be missed, but this will leave a few treasures in store for anyone who wishes to take the study of butterflies a little further.

The South American Swallowtails have one very predominant group, the Black *Papilios*, whose basic rounded shape is rather characteristic. Their size varies to some extent and their markings are in the form of patches of colour, which are often very vivid indeed, especially in the males. A female of *P.*

zacynthus is illustrated on page 45. A few species are very strongly mimetic (*P. pausanias* copies a steel-blue and yellow Heliconiid and *P. euterpinus* has precisely the same red-banded black as *Pereute*, a Pierid). Swordtail *Papilios* include white species banded with black as in *P. protesilaus* and quite a few others, yellow species like *P. thyastes* and the more neutral-coloured *P. leucaspis* and *serville* which have very prominent long tails.

Many South American Pieridae are not conspicuous or colourful but some are interestingly mimetic, and the black and red *Pereute* species, which are reminiscent of the *Delias* from the Old World, are particularly attractive. There are three giant Brimstones, *menippe*, *clorinde* and *maerula*. The *Dismorphia* must be mentioned. This is a group of butterflies peculiar to South America, with long narrow forewings and huge bulbous hindwings that are quite out of proportion. They are related to the *Leptidea* (the Wood Whites) of Europe and almost every species is mimetic of either *Heliconius*, *Ithomia* or *Mechanitis*, changing not only their colouring and pattern to suit their model but in some cases also their wing shape which, for *Dismorphia*, must have taken some adaptation. So good is the mimicry that one even sees them wrongly placed in collections.

The *Erycinidae* have more than 1,000 species in South America and comparatively few elsewhere. They are small species, many with intricate and very delicate patterning and bright colours. Amongst these the metallic *Ancyluris* and the iridescent-tailed *Diorina* are well known.

Heliconiids are species with long, narrow wings, which are found only in this region. They are strongly mimetic of each other and of the allied *Mechanitis*. Together they form a large group of species and are very abundant in certain areas.

One of the most important families of all is the Morphidae. The intense metallic blue of the males of many *Morphos* is quite unmatched by any other butterflies in the world. The smallest is *Morpho aega* with a wingspan of some 10 cm and they range up to the large *Morpho didius*, which has enormous iridescent blue wings. The females are duller shades of browns and yellows but still interesting. The *Morphos* of the *achilles* group have black wings with a broad band of pale iridescent blue or violet down each pair of wings. There are many species and forms of this type. A few, like *M. hercules* and *perseus* have shades of brown in both sexes and another group, which includes *catenarius* and *polyphemus*, has papery wings coloured greenish white and with markings in black.

Only in South America are found the amazing Brassolidae which mainly comprise the Owl butterflies or *Caligo* species. One of these appears on page 41. The upper sides of *Caligos* are often shot with beautiful purples and mauves or blues. They are a large species, ranging from 12 to 20 cm across.

The range of Satyridae, or Browns, is very large and many are very beautiful. Indeed, they could form the subject of a special study. A tropical species, *Callitaera aurorina*, has almost totally transparent wings, but there is a profusion of cerise scaling on the hindwings which makes it especially unusual and beautiful.

Ithomia, a tribe of Danaids, is extremely common. It is a distasteful group which both mimics and is mimicked. There are so many similar species and in such profusion that one cannot help wondering how the males of one species manage to recognize the females of their own kind.

South American Nymphalidae include some really spectacular species of which perhaps the *Agrias* are the kings. These

butterflies are robust like *Charaxes* and brilliantly coloure with intensely iridescent purples, blues, reds and greens in th most exotic combinations imaginable. The related *Preponas* a mostly black, banded with iridescent greeny-blue, and tw species are so fine that they look like *Agrias*. The *Callithe* species are smaller, but similarly coloured with the riche possible hues of deep blue, purple and green. Matching these b with greater diversity of colour are the *Catagrammas*, whic have intricate patterns on the under sides, as do the related a numerous species of *Callicore*, some of whose patterns actual resemble numerals. *Catagramma* upper sides vary greatly wi the species, but all are bright and some are intensely iridescen

evious pages, left: *Morpho epistrophus
olajewna* is one of the white *Morphos*.
is a Brazilian species and this is one of
rarest forms. It is a fast flier, found
t only in forest regions but also in open
untry, and it is capable of flying long
tances. A similar and closely related
ecies, *Morpho polyphemus*, is found as
north as Mexico, together with
other form of the white Morphos,
luna. Epistrophus measures about
cm across.

evious pages, right: The huge underside
e spots of the Owl butterfly give this
uth American species its name. When
wings are in set position and when it is
ld as illustrated, head downwards, its
eness to the head of an owl is very
iking. The butterfly holds its wings
ite differently when resting in a natural
sition and it is evident that it is not
itating an owl; if it is disturbed,
wever, it suddenly flinches, flapping
great wings (15 to 20 cm across), and
se terrifying eye spots are enough to

startle any predator, giving the butterfly
time to escape. The Owl is a member of a
big group of *Caligo* species, many of
which have beautiful iridescent
uppersides. Unique to South America
the larvae feed mostly on banana leaves.

Top left: The South American *Heliconius*
butterflies are one of the most important
groups found in the region and they do
not occur outside the American continent.
Heliconius wingspans range from 5 cm to
9 cm and each species has a very typical
long, narrow wing shape. This species is
Heliconius hydara, which was
photographed in Trinidad. It very much
resembles a commoner species,
H. melpomone.

Below left: Another very attractive
Heliconius is this species from Central
America known as *Heliconius sara.* The
iridescent blue changes position on the
wings according to the angle from which
they are viewed. There is a whole group

of species with this yellow-banded blue
or black colouring and *H. sara* with its red
spotting on the underside, is one of the
loveliest. The larvae of the Heliconiids
mostly have branched spines like the
European Vanessids and they can be
raised on the leaves of the passion plant
(*Passiflora*).

Above: The Gulf Fritillary, *Dione
vanillae*, is found over most of tropical
South America, throughout Central
America, and in the southern United
States. It is not a true Fritillary but its
orange colouring with black markings and
especially the silver-spangled underside is
reminiscent of the true Fritillaries.
D. vanillae is a species that breeds
especially well in captivity. The larvae
are spined like the Vanessids and striped
in a bright reddish-brown colour, with
quite a shiny skin. They feed on the leaves
of passion plant, which can be grown
outside the tropics and even, in sheltered
spots, out of doors.

Following pages: The depth of metallic iridescent blue all over its wings makes *Morpho rhetenor* incomparable with any other butterfly. It is one of an important family of *Morphos* found only in South America. The males of many *Morpho* species have some shade of iridescent blue all over, others have bands of blue on black and yet another group is an exquisite mother-of-pearl all over. The females of the blue species are usually gregarious but little is recorded about their life history and food plants. *Rhetenor* measures a good 18 cm across and the wingspans of other species range from 8 cm up to 25 cm or even more in the case of *Morpho hecuba*, which is not one of the blue species.

Above: *Morpho achillaena anakreon*, one of the Achilles group of *Morphos*, has broader bands of iridescent blue than most of the other forms and is shinier. This particular butterfly emerged from the chrysalis in less than five minutes. The chrysalis of *Morphos* is peculiarly large and bulbous, especially considering the rather small body of the butterfly. On emergence the butterfly ejects a large quantity of meconium, a waste fluid, and the body at once shrinks from a large, bloated sack to its normal size. The butterflies live in forests, flying near to the ground rather than high up like many of the other *Morphos*, and they do not travel long distances. This butterfly measures some 15 cm across.

Right: In South America there is a very large family known to entomologists as Black Swallowtails. This is *Papilio zacynthus polymetus*, a race found in the north of Brazil in the region of Pernambuco. The Black Swallowtails feed almost exclusively on *Aristolochia*, the group of tropical vines that are also important food plants for many of the Papilios in Asian and Australian jungles. The males of these *Papilios* are often more colourful than the females and both sexes are hard to identify unless one is a specialist because there are so many species and forms which are extremely similar. *Polymetus* has a wingspan of 10 cm.

Left: This is *Mechanitis polymnia*, one of a large group in the family Danaidae. It occurs throughout America from California southwards to Argentina, but it is mainly a tropical species and this particular specimen comes from the Lower Amazon. In some seasons *Mechanitis* are so prolific that they literally cover the bushes as they rest at night. They are extremely variable and many species have similar colouring, which makes identification very difficult; to make matters worse there is often hybridization in the wild, so it is difficult to be sure which *Mechanitis* has been found unless the markings are completely typical of a species. *Mechanitis* range in size from 4 cm to 8 cm.

Below: A common South American Swallowtail is this *Papilio (Battus) polydamas*. It is also found in the southern parts of North America.

Everywhere it prefers open country to forest and may be looked for on any waste ground where *Aristolochia* vines, its larval food plants, grow. *Polydamas* also likes farms and any cultivated land. The pupa is prettily shaped with flatte: humps on the abdomen. It may be bro or green. The wingspan ranges from 8 to 10 cm.

Below right: This is another large and beautiful Swallowtail, *Papilio thoas*, which is also quite a common species, especially in the most tropical regions. There are at least seven named forms. The form *cinyras* is one of the most colourful and consequently most often found in collections. *Thoas* is a very powerful flier, often soaring to great heights. It is found in open country, fields and gardens and its eggs are laid on citrus, which is the food plant of th caterpillar. This species has even been

...corded as far north as Texas. The ...ingspan varies but averages about ...5 cm.

...ight: European entomologists are ...miliar with Hairstreaks that have a ...ingspan of 2 cm to 3 cm but this exotic ...eauty from Ecuador, *Thecla coronata*, ...easures nearly 6 cm. The underside is ...lustrated here because of its very ...nusual pattern and coloration but the ...pperside is also beautifully coloured in ...idescent pale blue. The tails of these ...airstreaks serve a useful and interesting ...nction: the butterfly nearly always ...ights with its head downwards and tails ...rojecting upwards. A characteristic ...uffling movement of the hindwings ...uses the tails to waggle as if they were ...ntennae, hence a predator can easily ...onfuse the tail end with the head. If the ...il is pecked off no real harm comes to ...e butterfly, and it quickly escapes.

Left: *Formosissima* means 'the most beautiful' and can certainly be ranked among the most beautiful butterflies in the world. The *Ancyluris* genus is in the family Erycinidae, which has hundreds of species in South America, and is quite closely related to the European Duke of Burgundy Fritillary. All the *Ancyluris* have brilliant iridescent colouring, usually with a ground colour of dark blue. Their wing shape is characteristic of the genus and they measure less than 4 cm across. The underside of *formosissima*, a Peruvian species, has broad bands of iridescent bright carmine, which makes it very hard to decide which side to exhibit in a collection.

Below left: To collectors this attractive butterfly is one of the most famous in the world, greatly prized by anyone who is lucky enough to obtain a specimen. This is *Catopsilia avellaneda*, which is found in Cuba and nowhere else. The male is illustrated here but the female, though quite differently marked, is just as beautiful. The *Catopsilias* are a genus of normally common butterflies which migrate in large swarms, occurring both in the Old and the New World. They are attracted to moist patches and to dead animals or rotting fish. The larvae feed on *Cassia*, a genus of leguminous shrubs found in many parts of the tropics. *Catopsilia avellaneda* has a wingspan of 8 cm.

South American butterflies
1 *Agrias sardanapalus*, one of several richly coloured *Agrias* in America
2 *Prepona* species, a group of robust butterflies, which mostly have the same iridescent blue-green band on black
3 *Diorina dysoni*, a brilliantly coloured Erycinid   4 A *Eunica* species, one of several brilliant blue or purply species
5 *Catacore kolyma* is related to *Callicore* and shares its characteristic underside markings   6 *Calycopis demonassa*, a tiny Lycaenid   7 The famous and very rare *Papilio homerus*, found only in Jamaica   8 *Eurema elathea*, a Pierid, one of the Grass Yellows   9 A fine Hairstreak, *Thecla imperialis*, shown from the underside   10 *Colias vautheri*, one of the very few *Colias* in South America
11 A lovely Erycinid, *Lyropteryx apollonia*   12 *Callitaera aurorina*, is one of the transparent Satyrids and quite the prettiest   13 *Morpho portis*, an unusual shade of iridescent blue   14 *Catagramma cynosura*, the form from Brazil, as its name indicates is of worldwide renown.

Asian Butterflies

Asia forms an interesting transition from European an Palearctic butterflies, running right across from Turkey an Syria through India and China to the East Indian Islands, whe the fauna changes to that of the Australian region. As a co tinent, therefore, Asia has a very wide selection to offer, wi tremendous interest for entomologists and collectors.

In the tropics the *Papilios* are busy mimicking each othe producing forms that are very convincing. *Papilio polytes* and *memnon* are particularly polymorphic, producing both taile and tailless forms often in imitation of distasteful *Aristolochi* feeding Swallowtails. Other mimics include a remarkably goo imitation by *Papilio paradoxa* of the purple *Euploeas*, and t *Euploeas* are also copied by the Palm Flies, *Elymnias*, whic have other forms that are brown and mimic *Lymnas chrysippu* The Asian mimetic forms are very fascinating, though not numerous as those found in Africa.

In Asia Minor and the Middle East, the climate is mainly h and the terrain dusty and stony. Butterflies here are natural sparser than in the greener areas, but alongside the species whic

rmally tend to be common ones, there are also some which
e either scarce or extremely local, found almost exclusively in
ese parts. As one travels eastwards towards the mountains of
rsia and even higher into Afghanistan there appear new
ecies and local forms. This is an area of great interest to
tomologists and here, quite as much as in unexplored jungle
eas, it is possible that new species may yet be found. There are
me exceptionally interesting and beautiful *Colias* (Clouded
ellows), Satyrids, Blues and Parnassiids. In fact the whole area
om Afghanistan, stretching across north India to the Hima-
vas, is a mecca for the rarest and most diverse *Parnassius* or
pollo species. Here are the rare *charltonius*, *imperator* and
tocrator, large species with bizarre colouring in reds, oranges
d blues on a background of white. Commoner species abound
numerous forms which are extremely localized. The Pamirs in
uthern Russia are situated at a point where no less than five
untries (China, India, Pakistan, Russia and Kashmir) meet.
e political differences that exist greatly add to the compli-
tions of travelling in this remote area, and much work remains

to be done to study the butterflies of this fascinating region.

Russia is so large that it could be treated as a separate continent. Although it falls entirely within the Palearctic region, the
butterflies of the west are mid-European and there is a gradual
transition travelling eastwards, through the butterflies of Asia
Minor in southern Russia (in the north, although at equivalent
longitudes the butterfly fauna is still European or, especially in
Siberia, Arctic) until, passing through Siberia to Mongolia, one
meets the more northerly Chinese butterfly fauna, which finally
meets that of Japan.

The butterflies of China are also transitional and include
both tropical and temperate species according to latitude.
Shanghai's commonest species include such species as Brimstone, Small Copper, Green-veined White and Painted Lady,
together with *Papilio xuthus*, *Sericinus telamon* and a few other
subtropical species. Only 10 degrees further south is Hong Kong
where the commonest species include *Eurema hecabe*, *Danaus*,
Euploea, *Melanitis*, *Neptis*, *Catopsilia* and *Hebomoia glaucippe*,
all of which are truly tropical species.

The island of Taiwan is famous for its butterflies which are unique in that they form part of its export industry. This quite small island has a superabundance of butterflies in hundreds of species and despite the collection of millions each year, they keep appearing each new season. There is concern about this for fear the existence of the butterflies could be in danger, but it is remarkable that nature seems to balance itself again each year and there is not at the moment any noticeable decline caused by this collecting. Taiwan is rich in beautiful *Papilionidae*, which are mainly tropical. An outstanding one is *Atrophaneura horishanus*, which is all black with deep magenta in large patches on the under side hindwings. There are two black and yellow Birdwings, *Troides aeacus* and the rarer *T. magellanus*.

Although farther north than Taiwan, Japan has species that are tropical and subtropical as well as a wide range of species that are comparable to or identical with European ones. There are many geographical forms or allied species of Fritillaries and other Nymphalidae but one of the most interesting groups are the very large and colourful Hairstreaks, for which Japan is renowned. Many have shimmering green or ultramarine covering the entire surface of the wings.

In northern India butterflies are most plentiful and this region is famous for the Bhutan Glory and the magnificent green, tailed *Teinopalpus imperialis*. These are true Asian butterfly fauna. The drier and less green areas of central India have fewer butterflies and in the south are a few species which could be considered as belonging to Ceylon, species such as *Papilio*

hector and *Delias eucharis*. Ceylon has developed many species of its own, as for instance, the blue Leaf butterfly, *Kallima phillarchus*, the Blue Mormon, *Papilio polymnestor* and other unique to the island. The butterflies of north India are mostly found in Burma also, and so are some that are usually considered chiefly as Chinese. As one travels down the peninsula into Malaysia the Indian fauna changes (noticeably in Thailand) to that of Malaysia with many new species and only the commoner Indian ones in addition.

Malaysia has the Rajah Brooke's Birdwing, which occurs as a rarity in Thailand and is also found in Borneo, with a subspecies on the island of Sumatra. Other striking Malaysian butterflies found on the mainland and surrounding islands include the Orange Albatross, a Pierid, *Papilio coon*, which has extraordinarily narrow wings and bulbous tails, *nox*, a black species that is uncommon, and many others, making this a unique region. Here are found half a dozen more Birdwings — the black and yellow *Troides*. Java and the other Indonesian islands also carry Malaysian fauna and at their eastern limits there are signs of another change to the Australian fauna. The Philippines form the eastern limit of Asian fauna, and have some species that are unique to this group of islands. A *Trogonoptera*, relative of Rajah Brooke's Birdwing, known as *trojanus*, lives on Palawan and *Papilio rumanzovia* (a marvellous scarlet and black species) and *P. kotzebuea* are found only here. There is also the endemic *Troides rhadamantus*. *Troides magellanus* lives here, and is otherwise known to occur only on a tiny island south of Taiwan.

evious pages, **left**: The chrysalis of most
the *Euploea* or Crow butterflies looks
ore like a shining artificial Christmas
ee bauble than the natural pupa of a
tterfly. It shines like polished metal,
such an extent that you can actually
e yourself in it. Very often there is a
rong electric blue iridescence and the
verall colour is very variable indeed.
he caterpillar is attractively ringed and
as four pairs of antennae-like filaments;
ese are found on many Danaid larvae.
he caterpillar feeds on milkweeds,
eander and species of *Ficus*, the fig
mily.

evious pages, **right**: Like most of the
row butterflies, which are found only in
e Old World, *Euploea core* is very dark,
eming almost all black, but in certain
ghts there is a deep velvety blue or
rple iridescence. These *Euploea*
tterflies are related to the milkweed-
eding butterflies: they fly with a slow,
ting flight and look as if they might be

weak, though in fact they are extraordinarily tenacious of life and recover
from being stunned more than any other
kind of butterfly. They are poisonous
and if attacked, they feign death and
ooze out droplets of poisonous fluid from
the thorax. The males project long and
very pretty brushes from the tail which
are scented and are used in the courtship
flight to attract the female.

Above left: Although not colourful this
butterfly, *Hestia leuconoë*, is one of the
most impressive of any in the world, not
only for its size (15 cm to 20 cm) but
because of the curious papery texture of
its wings and the bold and interesting
pattern in black and white. It is reported
that native children use dead specimens
as kites because of their durable texture
and the way they can be made to glide
through the air. *Leuconoë* is a Danaid
with several geographical races, occurring
mainly in China and Taiwan. Throughout
Southeast Asia and the Australian islands

are quite a number of *Hestia* species (also
known as *Idea*), all with the instantly
recognizable patterning in black and
white, many of them even larger than
leuconoë.

Above: The Far Eastern *Kaniska canace*
is closely related to the European
Tortoiseshells and Commas and this can
be seen especially from its wing shape and
texture. It is reasonably common and
widely distributed from India to China,
Japan, Malaysia and the Philippines. The
butterfly breeds mainly in wooded areas
and is found also in gardens and orchards.
It is attracted to fruit as well as flowers,
but above all to exuding tree sap, where
it rests with wings closed so that only the
dark camouflaged surface is visible and
the butterfly seems to melt into the
background of tree bark. The caterpillar
is orange with black spots and yellow
branched spines with black tips. It feeds
on *Smilax china*, a thorny climber with
red berries. The wingspan is about 6 cm.

Left: Known as the Sun butterfly, this *Delias aglaia* is a distant relative of the European Whites and a member of a large group of *Delias* found over most of Asia and especially in New Guinea and the Australian region. They are all highly colourful on the underside with the upperside mainly white, patterned with black. Most species feed on *Loranthus*, species of mistletoe, which occur all over the Asian tropics. The larvae live gregariously and, curiously, all pupate together with perhaps as many as 20 or 30 pupae on one stem. It was from one of these stems that this butterfly emerged and was photographed in Hong Kong: sometimes you will even find the butterflies all hanging together drying their wings.

Centre: A classic example of camouflage is this famous Indian Leaf butterfly, *Kallima inachus*. The underside pattern includes a central line in imitation of the leaf's midrib, with veins leading off it. The whole shape of the wings is like a leaf and there is even a tail which looks like the stalk. The markings and ground colour are infinitely variable, imitating the different stages of incipient decay. When disturbed the butterfly darts off and quickly settles, often on the ground where it immediately disappears from view amongst the vegetation. As well as *inachus* there are other *Kallimas* in Ceylon, Malaysia and other regions, some with blue on the upperside in place of the orange of *inachus*.

Below left: Some of the *Delias* butterflies are found in colonies, with sometimes up to 100 flying round one bush or tree. They can often be found like this in Java, although there are relatively few species of *Delias* there. This lovely *Delias belisama* usually lives singly and is one of the less common species. This picture was taken in the world-famous botanical gardens at Bogor, a few miles south of Djakarta. The bright flowers attract many wild butterflies and some of the scarcer and particularly pretty species come into the gardens from the surrounding wilder regions.

Far right: The Lacewing butterflies of India, China and the Australian region are some of the most beautiful species in the area. This one is *Cethosia biblis* from Hong Kong, where it is very rare; it is more commonly met with in India. The name Lacewing comes from the intricate pattern and beautiful edging on the underside. The upperside is just as beautiful, and this is shown for *Cethosia chrysippe* from Australia (the prettiest of all *Cethosias*) on page 68. The larvae feed on passion plant and live gregariously. Clustered together they look very striking as they are spiny and have coloured rings all down their bodies. The eggs are laid in batches, each carefully deposited a measured distance

from the next like pins in a bowling alley.

Above right: This lovely Nymphalid from Hong Kong, *Symbrenthia hippoclus*, has just emerged from the chrysalis and shows the beautiful texture of an absolutely fresh butterfly before it has flown. *Hippoclus* is quite a rarity in Hong Kong but it is found right across the Asian region from India to China and Malaysia and even farther east to New Guinea. The larvae live in a gregarious colony and the pupae, each of which is suspended from the tail, look a little like those of the Small Tortoiseshell.

Right: This female *Apatura parisatis staurakius* is more attractive than the male, which is almost black all over. *Apatura* is the same genus as the famous Purple Emperor but this Hong Kong species is a good deal smaller, only about 4 cm across. *Parisatis* is quite a common species found in Ceylon, India, Malaysia and south China. It lives in wooded areas and has a quick flight, settling on leaves with its wings stretched wide open to bask in the sunlight. The larva is green with a yellow stripe down the back and two black horns. It lives on species of *Celtis* (Nettle tree).

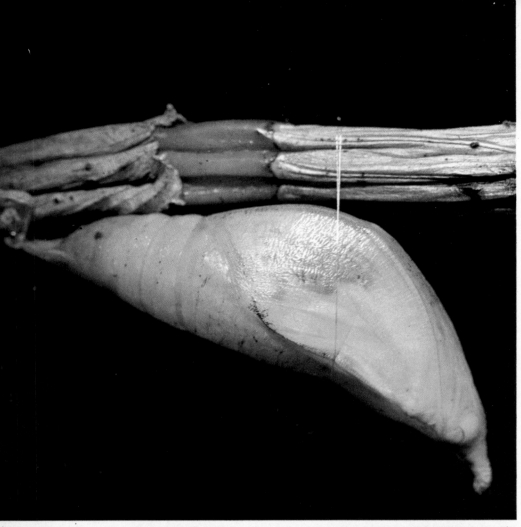

Left: The future markings of the butter are just showing through the chrysalis case of this Giant Orange Tip, *Hebomo glaucippe*, from China. The pupa measures nearly 4 cm and the resulting butterfly is a real giant by European Orange Tip standards, a good 10 cm across. It is one of the largest Pieridae in the world, white with orange-tipped forewings and on the underside hindwi a pale-brown camouflage pattern. The larvae feed on species of *Capparis*. *Glaucippe* is a common species throughout the Far East and has relate and beautiful yellow forms and species in the East Indian Islands.

Below left: *Papilio memnon* is one of Asia's largest Swallowtails, measuring some 12 cm or more across. Illustrated here is the female, which occurs in seve quite different forms, often with long spatulate tails as in the form *distantian* found in Taiwan. The male is much plainer, never tailed, with an almost uniform, slightly iridescent, gun metal blue over all four wings. Both are a wonderful sight when several are feedir from a flowery tropical shrub such as *Lantana*, constantly on the move, hovering gracefully from one flower to the next. *Memnon* is found right across Asia and is common in most of the tropical regions.

Right: The caterpillar of *Papilio memn* is so similar in appearance to many oth *Papilio* larvae that it is difficult to tell from another. This is particularly curio when you compare the resulting butterflies, which look so entirely different. Examples include the black and yellow *P. demoleus* and *demodocu* and the black and white *polytes*. When younger the *memnon* caterpillar is blackish with white areas and an oily skin, looking just like a bird dropping. If disturbed the larva produces a red forked organ from behind its head whi emits a strong smell that remains in the air for some time. This is found in mos Swallowtail larvae as a protection again predators.

Below: Rajah Brooke's Birdwing, *Trogonoptera brookiana*, is one of the most famous butterflies in the world and is grouped with the magnificent Birdwings of New Guinea. *Brookiana* comes only from the Malaysian region. The males cluster on river banks to take moisture and in certain clearings are found quite commonly. The female is seldom seen and much less common but this must partly be that she keeps to the tops of the trees and is more difficult to reach. The larvae probably feed on *Aristolochia*.

Bottom: The tails on this unusual Papilionid, *Lamproptera meges*, are disproportionately long and very unusual. *Lamproptera* is found primarily in India and Malaysia, but also as rather a rarity

in Hong Kong. It lives in places where there is running water, usually occurring singly. When flying, and even when settled, its wings vibrate so quickly that they seem to be just a bluish haze. The wingspan of this small butterfly is about 4 cm yet its length, with tails, is nearly 8 cm.

Below right: This tropical Skipper. *Bibasis gomata*, is an exception in that it is active at night and hides by day. It comes from Hong Kong and is found also in northern India. The upper side is a uniform, slightly iridescent grey-green and this beautifully rayed underside is distinctive of the species amongst hundreds of allied Skippers. The pupa is white, spotted with black and the larva also is

white with black markings. It feeds on *Horsfieldia* and other Asian plants. *Gomata*'s wingspan is more than 4 cm.

Right: This caterpillar of *Papilio aristolochiae*, which was bred in England on *Aristolochia tagala*, is so like the larva of the East Indian Birdwing that it is easy to see the relationship of the two butterflies which, as adults, look totally dissimilar. This caterpillar is about 3 cm long, while that of a Birdwing might be 8 cm or 9 cm long and very fat. *Papilio aristolochiae*, the Common Rose, is a species found from India and Ceylon throughout Asia to China, but not into New Guinea. It is a dark velvety brown with large rose-coloured spots on the hindwings and a large white central area.

Above: Probably Asia's commonest Swallowtail is this Common Bluebottle, *Papilio sarpedon*. It is one of the Kite Swallowtails or *Graphium* species. From India and Ceylon eastwards, *sarpedon* is found in every country very abundantly and in several geographical races which affect its colouring and pattern. This Malaysian form of *sarpedon, luctatius* is quite the loveliest with rich greeny-blue colouring and only thin bars across the windowed forewings. The butterfly flies with a very nervous motion, seldom actually resting but seeming to pause at a flower, dancing all over it with its wings perpetually beating. The larvae feed on Lauracae, cinnamon and custard apple.

Asian butterflies
1 & 2 Male and female of the Japanese Hairstreak, *Chrysozephyrus ataxus*
3 A tailed *Arophala* species, one of scores of species found in forests throughout tropical Asia, mostly brilliantly coloured
4 A long-tailed Hairstreak from Malaysia, *Eooxylides tharis*   5 A Formosan Lycaenid, *Horagia rarasana*   6 The rare *Espasia forsteri* from Formosa   7 An *Anteros* species, with a remarkable underside pattern   8 *Papilio karna*, one of the finest Asian Swallowtails, from Java   9 A strange *Catopsilia* which looks like two halves of different butterflies put together. This is *C. sylla* from Java
10 The world-renowned Bhutan Glory, *Armandia lidderdalei*, from northern India
11 *Colias olga*, found in the Caucasus and one of the most richly orange of all *Colias*   12 *Leudorfia puziloi*, a Papilionid from Japan   13 *Dercas verhuelli* from Borneo, a vivid Pierid
14 *Archon apollinus*, an *Aristolochia* feeder from Turkey   15 *Papilio paradoxa* form *telearchus*, a classic mimic of No 16   16 *Euploea midamus*
17 Probably the smallest butterfly in the world, a *Cupido* species

Butterflies of the Australian Region

As well as the Australian continent this region includes New Zealand, New Guinea and all its surrounding islands from Celebes (Sulawesi) to the Solomon Isles. Because of the tremendous number of islands this area has many hundreds of adapted geographical or island forms of species which have developed independently and make it a region of exceptional interest to the entomologist. New Zealand has only about a dozen species of its own but these are interesting and mostly unique to that country. It is thought that they are more ancient in origin than the Australian species, which may have been affected by the encroachment, over millions of years, of butterflies from the Indian and Malaysian region. Celebes is a transitional island where there is influence from both Malaysian and Australian forms, yet they are in many cases forms that are found only in Celebes. The numerous islands between Celebes and New Guinea contain many exciting species and forms that are unique. Some of these islands are tiny and it is amazing to realize that prominent species amongst world lepidoptera can occur only in such minute and possibly precarious colonies. The

una of the tropical islands is incredibly rich but it thins out as he moves further south. Queensland, being tropical, has a wealth of species but Western Australia and South Australia have more temperate climates and many fewer species. Tasmania, to the extreme south, has under 40.

While only some of the wealth of exciting species can be discussed here, the rest can be followed up in some of the excellent recent publications. The Birdwings, one of the greatest wonders of the whole animal kingdom, nearly all come from this region. The finest species are all uncommon or extremely rare and are protected by law. On the Solomon Isles lives Queen Victoria's Birdwing, *Ornithoptera victoriae*, and *O. allotei*, of which fewer than six have ever been seen. Both are magnificent species with markings in iridescent greens, blues, yellows and golds. The blue *O. urvillianus* comes from there also and its close relative, *O. lydius*, which has the same shape and pattern but in black and gold, comes from the opposite side of New Guinea, on Halmahera. Two other Birdwings with the same patterning are *croesus*, a paler gold species from Bachan near

Halmahera, and the beautiful green and black *priamus*. *Priamus* is an important species as it is by far the most widespread and occurs on many islands and in many named geographical forms, including three in Australia itself. The commonest is form *poseidon*, found over much of the New Guinea mainland. In addition to these there are seven other extremely rare and extraordinarily beautiful species found in New Guinea: *Ornithoptera alexandrae*, the largest of all (the female is nearly 25 cm across); *paradisea* whose hindwings terminate in wisp-like curved tails; *meridionalis*, which is somewhat similar, coloured in shining gold and metallic lime green; *rothschildi*, unlike any other species; *tithonus*; *chimaera*; and *goliath*. These species look quite unreal and to see one flying wild is one of the most exciting experiences of a lifetime. There are other species of the *Troides* tribe, the black and yellow Birdwings found also in this region.

Swallowtails abound. Many are species for the experts, not all so attractive to look at and some of them difficult to separate and name, but here too are some of the world's loveliest

species. *Papilio blumei* from Celebes is a large Swallowtail, iridescent green almost all over with its tails clear shining blue. *Papilio ulysses*, the Blue Mountain Swallowtail, is found over almost the whole of this tropical region; a miniature of it called *montrouzieri* comes from New Caledonia. Two beautiful green Swallowtails are *P. lorquinianus* from West Irian and Halmahera and *P. pericles*, green, merging into blue and purple, from Timor. Exclusive to the Australian tropics is the large round-winged yellow and black *Papilio euchenor* which eludes capture by darting amongst the jungle creepers where it is impossible to wield a net. The Swallowtail by the strange name *Cressida cressida cressida* reminds one of *Parnassius* with its transparent forewings; the female is almost totally transparent. She even forms a pouch on the abdomen after pairing as the Apollos do. There is a large family of butterflies in the same group as *aegeus*, *ambrax* and *fuscus*. These are all citrus feeders and subject to great variation. The *Graphium* or Swordtail species include a famous New Guinea butterfly, *Papilio weiskei*, which is delicately coloured with greens and a clear lilac; it has a rarer relative *stresemanni*. *P. codrus*, a large-tailed species, is spectacular and very varied in colouring.

The Pieridae excel themselves in this region. The *Delias* butterflies are unbelievably beautiful. But the finest species are often in inaccessible parts or on small islands and hence are seldom seen in collections. From the islands west of New Guinea comes the superb yellow Giant Orange Tip, *H. leucippe* and local forms of *H. glaucippe* also. One of the *Catopsilias*, *C. scylla*, has yellow hindwings and white forewings as if a joker had stuck two halves of different butterflies together.

There are many Danaids in this region well worth studying. The *Euploeas* are most numerous and include spectacular species like the giant blue *callithoë* and the unusual white or which looks like an aberration, *E. phenareta.*

Among the Nymphalidae (which are very numerous indee brilliant luminous violets, blues and pinks are found in *Terin* species from New Guinea, and in *Cirrochroa regina* and *imper trix* from the islands of Aru and Biak. *Cethosia* produces a unusual species, *lechenaulti* from Timor, reminiscent of tl Camberwell Beauty with its yellow border on dark brow. *Mynes* are Nymphalids with very much the colouring of *Delia* a strange example of what must be mimicry. *Hypolimnas* hav many species in this region and a striking giant species *pandarus* from the isles of Serang and Ambon, close to Ne Guinea. *Kallima*, the Leaf butterflies, do not extend to th region but are replaced by the genus *Doleschallia* that is al very leaflike and a little smaller. There are no *Charaxes* bi some *Polyura* which are closely allied to them. *Libythea* he has lovely purple forms. These are the Snout butterflies, Lib theidae, a family on their own and present on every continent.

Among the other butterflies we must not pass over tl numerous *Taenaris*, nearest relatives of the *Morphos*, which a white with yellow-ringed eye spots and the *Elymnias* (Satyri which mimic both these and the *Euploeas*. Amongst the ve numerous and richly coloured Lycaenidae are magnificent Ha streaks and the especially Australian *Ogyris*, which live in asso ation with ants. Strangest of all is the genus *Liphyra*, the bigge Lycaenid in the world (nearly 10 cm) whose caterpillar lives tree ants' nests, feeding on their brood, and protecting itself t living within an impregnable hard outer casing that it has bu for itself. It also has a self-made escape system for when emerges, preventing the angry ants from dragging it back whe it is still soft and vulnerable.

evious pages, left: This little Satyrid, *riexenica kershawi*, is found only in *stern Victoria in Australia. The genus *confined to Southeastern Australia and *smania and the species all have the *me general colouring and pattern, *sembling a rather small Wall Brown *ararge megera*). In parts *Oriexenica* is *uite common, living in grassy areas, *ainly on mountains and on high ground. *e butterflies are attracted to fireweed, *oundsel and other nectar-bearing *owers. The food plant of the caterpillar *a local grass known as wire grass, *trarrhena.*

evious pages, top right: Related to the *onarch, this *Lymnas chrysippus* is *own as the Plain Tiger in some *untries but in Australia, where this *bspecies *petilia* comes from, it is called *e Lesser Wanderer. *Chrysippus* is *ographically very variable (with very *arked differences in Africa) and this *ustralian form has especially dark *orders with a distinctive scorched *ging. It is quite common over most *' Australia and at times is found even *ep inside major towns. This distasteful *anaid is mimicked especially by the *ymphalid *Hypolimnas misippus*. *rysippus* larvae feed on *Asclepias *d can easily be reared in temperate *untries.

evious pages, right: This is the female *Hypolimnas misippus*, the Danaid Egg *ly. Since she has to carry the eggs and *s to get around to disperse them over *e countryside, it is she who resembles *chrysippus* most. *Misippus* is found *roughout the tropical parts of the *ustralian region. It prefers the edges of *in forest but is often attracted into *rdens. Outside Australia this species *found in a wide band sweeping *estwards across tropical Asia and *frica into South America.

eft: The male of *Hypolimnas misippus *not mimetic (though there might be *onsidered some resemblance to the *uploeas*) and he is so unlike the female *at they seem to be quite different *ecies. The males are territorial, *trolling their particular area with *eat vigour and chasing off any intruding *utterflies, just as certain birds do. One *od plant of *misippus* which can be *own in Europe is *Portulaca*, but *nfortunately this species is not one *at is normally available to breeders. *isippus* is about 7 cm across.

op right: From some of the remotest *rts of New Guinea comes this pretty *elias sagessa*. The life history of this *ecies appears not to be recorded but it *uite probably feeds, like most other *Delias*, *n mistletoes or *Loranthus*. Many of the *ghland *Delias* like *sagessa* are found in *oups on moist patches of soil and it is *ossible to find a number of different

species feeding together, but to get to such places it often requires several days' travelling from any form of civilization in lower areas. *Sagessa* has a wingspan of about 5 cm.

Above: Quite a common jungle forest butterfly is this Nymphalid, *Vindula arsinoë*. As well as in the Australian region *Vindula* occurs right across Asia. Known as the Cruiser, this butterfly has a swift flight, frequently soaring up high into the air and sailing down to perch for only a few moments before taking off again. The female is easily distinguished by prominent white banding on the forewings. She is larger than the male, measuring over 10 cm across. The larvae have typical Nymphalid branched spines and live on several tropical creepers, including *Passiflora*. The pupa has leaflike projections which make it look like a dead leaf caught up in the tendrils of the creeper.

Above: The Red Lacewing, *Cethosia chrysippe*, is a species found in Queensland and in New Guinea. To quote from Charles McCubbin, in his latest work *Australian Butterflies*, 'when these butterflies are flying in the sunshine the scarlet areas of the wings seem almost to catch fire and the dark wing-edges glow a deep and lustrous purple; a sight so splendid that I consider this species our most beautiful butterfly.' Although common in just a few localities *chrysippe* is quite a find and much admired by collectors. The larvae, which feed on a forest vine that looks much like *Passiflora*, are very spiny and conspicuously banded with yellow and black. The butterfly has a wingspan of nearly 9 cm.

Centre left: *Phalantha phalantha* is a tropical species, rather rare in Australia but common in New Guinea. It is found in Africa and right across the tropical regions of Asia into the Solomon Isles. The butterflies are sometimes found in clusters, not only in damp spots but sometimes for no apparently obvious reason at the side of a dry stony road. *Phalantha* is a Fritillary-like Nymphalid which measures nearly 6 cm across. It has an exceptionally pretty small green pupa, decorated with silver tubercles which are circled with red. The larvae ·feed on species of willow.

Left: Australia and New Guinea are rich in brilliantly coloured Lycaenidae and this is one of the tropical *Danis* species. There are some 50 species of *Danis* in the Australian region, mostly with the same general pattern on the underside, so it takes a specialist to identify them with certainty. On the upperside there is great

diversity of colouring and marking. The males are nearly always iridescent shad of blue, purple or mauve and the femal usually have heavy black markings with little blue or green. Most species averag about 4 cm across.

Top right: Throughout the tropics ther are species of *Eurema* like this one: the are known as the Common Grass Yello They fly in and around rain forest and dry scrub alike and even if there are no other butterflies some *Eurema* can usu be found. At times they swarm and it i common sight to find large clusters on damp river banks, sipping moisture. Almost all *Eurema* species are yellow with broad black borders but a few are white or have both colours. The larvae feed on Cruciferae, especially on *Cappa* These are small butterflies measuring from 1.5 to 3 cm.

Right: In New Guinea one of the most exciting sights is this Mountain Blue Swallowtail, *Papilio ulysses*. It is widespread but not a common species and not very often seen in dry weather. After the rains it is possible to find *ulysses* down on the ground taking moisture and this is how this butterfly was photographed while engrossed in drinking at a jungle clearing some 40 k from the capital, Port Moresby. If disturbed, *ulysses* is up and away out o sight in no time. It can be found also at the flowers of hibiscus, where the contrast of the scarlet flowers and the intense blue of *ulysses* is particularly striking. *Ulysses* is found also in northe Australia and in many geographical race in most of the islands round New Guine and in the Solomon Isles. It is a large species with a wingspan of 12 cm or mo

Left: The local name of this butterfly, *Delias mysis*, is the Union Jack. In Australia and New Guinea are found almost all the world's species of *Delias*: there are scores of these, including some very rare species from inaccessible parts of New Guinea. *Mysis* is one of the less rare species, which is found in Queensland and even more commonly in New Guinea. It often breeds on a species of *Loranthus*, a kind of mistletoe, which is parasitic of citrus orchards. It has large and broad leaves and is difficult to detect on an orange tree until its long tubular red flowers appear. The larvae of *mysis* are gregarious and so are the pupae.

Centre left: The female of *Ornithoptera priamus* is even larger than the male, reaching a wingspan of 25 to 28 cm. As with all the *Ornithoptera* the female is not brilliantly coloured but she is nonetheless very impressive. All of them, even the most exotic and rare species, are very similar in general colouring but there is tremendous variation in patterning and detailed coloration within any of the species, especially from one region to another. *Priamus* occurs in a number of distinct named forms, three of which are found in Australia. The larvae feed on species of *Aristolochia*.

Below: *Ornithoptera primus* is one of the famous Birdwings, the largest butterflies in the world and generally considered to be the most beautiful. Some species are now very rare indeed and are protected by law. The majority of these species come from New Guinea and the surrounding islands. *Priamus* is one of the less rare ones; in fact, it is possible to find places in New Guinea where 15 or more can be seen flying around a single tree. They are large, measuring 17 cm or more across (even larger specimens have been recorded) and they are an incredible sight soaring around looking for the females or

flying high up like birds above the tree canopy, feeding on the flowers of creepers. To either side of New Guinea are related races which, instead of bein green in colouring, are deep blue and black (from the Solomon Isles) or oran and black (from Halmahera).

Australian butterflies
1 *Ornithoptera paradisea* from New Guinea. With its exceptionally beautifu wing shape this must surely be one of t world's finest butterflies. It is found in several parts of New Guinea ranging fro the west to the east   2 *Ornithoptera alexandrae* Another very rare Birdwing with its own peculiar wing shape. It is rather variable in colouring, some male being very much bluer. The female, which is the largest butterfly in the world, is dark brown   3 *Ornithoptera goliath* Several forms of this magnificer gold and green species are found in sm isolated pockets in New Guinea. This butterfly is very rarely seen in collectic

Following page: *Papilio macleyanus* is only found in Australia. It is one of the *Graphium* species or Kite Swallowtails, and occurs in eastern Australia from north Queensland right down to Tasmania, where it is the only *Papilio* species. It is not found in South Austra or in the west. Generally this is a mountain butterfly but in some localit it is found at sea level. The larvae feed on sassafras and camphor laurel among other plants and they give off such a strong smell from the osmaterium if th are disturbed that they betray their presence if the food plant is shaken by a searcher. Like some other *Graphiums* the colour only comes to their wings at their emergence, when they are expose to sunlight. If they emerge in captivity without sun they will remain pale and without their proper colour. *Macleyan* measures 8 cm across.

1

2

3

Acknowledgments

The publishers would like to thank the following individuals and organizations for their kind permission to reproduce the pictures in this book:

F Baillie Natural History Photographic Agency 42, 43 top, 60, 66, 67 top.

Anthony Bannister N H P A   25, 30.

Dick Brown Natural Science Photos   24.

B D'Abrera Natural Science Photos   64, 70 bottom, 72.

Eric Elms N H P A   62, 65 bottom, 67 bottom, 68 top and bottom, 69 top, 70 top.

Robert Goodden Worldwide Butterflies Ltd   endpapers, 1-22, 26 bottom, 28 top, 31, 32, 33 bottom, 34, 35, 37, 38 top, 39, 40, 41, 43 bottom, 44-59, 60 centre, 61, 63, 65 top, 68 centre, 69 bottom, 70 centre, 71.

A B Klots   33 top, 36, 38 bottom.

J L Mason N H P A   23, 28 bottom.

Klaus Paysan Natural Science Photos   29 bottom.

J Seeley N H P A   36 centre.

P H Ward Natural Science Photos   26 top, 27, 29 top.

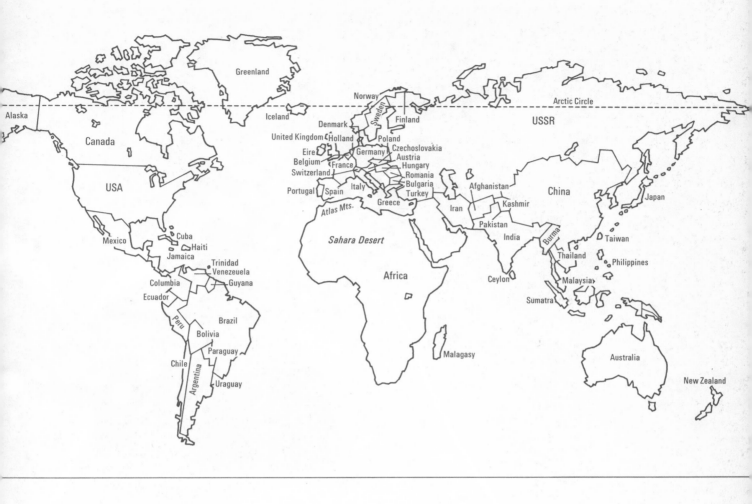